Praise for Living the Season Well

"*Living the Season Well* invites readers to slow down and make Christmas about presence instead of presents. Beginning with Advent and extending to Epiphany (and beyond), Jody explains the basic framework of the church calendar, provides historical context for many of our cultural traditions, and offers accessible suggestions to help family members of all ages shift their focus from consumerism to Christ. If you're ready for a frenzy-free holiday season infused with purpose and peace, this little book will show you how to start small and start now."

—Jeanne Damoff, Speaker, Workshop Leader, author of *Parting the Waters, Finding Beauty in Brokenness*

"I read this book during an especially busy season, when the last thing on my mind was Christmas. But when I finished the last page, I was shocked to discover that I could hardly wait for the season to arrive. Jody Collins is like a real-life, wide-eyed Christmas elf, helping you see the season the way God intended. *Living the Season Well* is full of inspiration, practical help, wisdom, and humor. It made me long for more of Jesus. This book is a delightful invitation to slow down and savor the season – and the Savior."

—Jennifer Dukes Lee, author of *The Happiness Dare* and *Love Idol*

"Simplify. Slow down. Savor. Set aside fatigue and commercial hype. Jody Collins has created a handbook of meaningful ways to celebrate "the arc of holy days from Advent through Epiphany." *Living the Season Well* brims with faith, daring, and practical inspiration to help Christian families honor Christmas. Affordable, adaptable ideas include fasting from noise, harnessing electronics for other-centered giving, and exploring ancient traditions, like chalking the door. The key? *Start small. Start now.*"

—Laurie Klein, author of poetry collection, *Where the Sky Opens* and classic praise chorus *"I Love You, Lord."*

"If you're anything like me (let's just say my family calls me the Grinch for good reason), you need Jody Collins to help you recalibrate your Christmas. Written with warmth, approachability and humor and filled with practical, applicable suggestions, *Living the Season Well* will guide you on a journey toward slowing down, simplifying and savoring the moments of the holiday season. This year, give *yourself* a gift, and let *Living the Season Well* shift your approach to Christmas from frenzied to fulfilled."

—Michelle DeRusha, author of *Katharina and Martin Luther: The Radical Marriage of a Runaway Nun and a Renegade Monk*

Living the Season Well

Reclaiming Christmas

Jody Lee Collins

Jody Collins for Sandy and family— God bless you! Dec. 2020 +

LIVING THE SEASON WELL: RECLAIMING CHRISTMAS

Second Edition

Copyright © 2018 by Jody Collins

All Rights Reserved Newport Press

www.jodyleecollins.com

Ultimate design, content, editorial accuracy and views expressed or implied in this work are those of the author

Cover Design by William E. G. Johnson (wegj@wegjart.com)
More brilliant illustrations at garrisonthestronghold.com

Back cover photo by Leah Abraham

Book layout by Clark Kenyon at Upwork

Feel free to quote up to 200 words in print or online with full citation and/or a hyperlink to the book at www.jodyleecollins.com/books. For longer quotations or multiple quotations, contact Jody at heyjode70@yahoo.com.

ISBN: 978-0-578-40362-5 (Paperback)
         978-0-578-40361-8 (eBook)

God became human in order that humans might participate in God...

—*Wendy Wright,* The Vigil: Keeping Watch in the Season of Christ's Coming

*For my children and grandchildren,
those in Heaven, those present and those to come,
the brightest stars in my world.*

Contents

Foreword

ONCE UPON A TIME, I WAS the grinch.

I didn't know I was the grinch, of course. I was mad at everyone *else* for stealing Christmas. The consumerism and consumption of the holidays made me angry. The busy whirl of parties, plans, presents, and all the rest of the supposed Christmas cheer wore me out. I dreaded Christmas.

The nadir struck the year my firstborn was two. He tore through the mound of gifts from his grandparents, aunts, uncles, and friends, literally ripping the paper off, glancing at the gift, chucking it over his shoulder, and lisping, "Is there another one?"

I sat dumbfounded at his ingratitude, even while I knew it was largely not his fault. The adults in his life had set him up for this selfish display. We were the ones who plied him with presents, who sat around in adoring delight as he tossed first one present and then the next aside as if this lavish outpouring of gifts was his due, his right.

For years, I had been trying to do Christmas differently, trying to get away from what seemed to me the obligatory passing around of money on December 25, with very little success. I irritated my family and my husband's family with my harping on the ills of consumerism and the anti-Christian focus of all this consumption. My mother and my mother-in-law, for whom gifts are a way of showing and receiving love, lovingly ignored me. Hence the giant pile of gifts for my soon-to-be-spoiled two-year-old.

Oh, how I wish I had had a book like *Living the Season Well* in those days. I needed help. I needed someone to show me what a long, slow Christmas might actually look like *in practice* (and not in the nebulous visions of perfection in my head!). I needed an older, wiser woman to gently counsel me not to waste my time criticizing customs that were meaningful to others even if they meant less than nothing to me. I needed Jody Collins to come alongside me and say, "Start slow. Start now. Choose one thing this year, another thing next year. In ten years, Christmas will look very different."

I did slowly figure it out for myself, through a lot of reading and a lot of mistakes. We never had a repeat of that Christmas 12 years ago, and slowly, year by year, we've made one or two changes at a time, such that now I actually look forward to December, to the tree and the garlands and the lights and my annual Christmas party. Yes. Every December for the past four years I, the former grinch, have thrown a party for a dozen of my favorite women—and I like it! If that's not proof of transformation, I don't know what is!

But you, gentle reader, don't have to figure it out on your own. You have Jody's kindly, humorous wisdom right here in these pages, and I am glad for you. My prayer for you is that

as you adopt or adapt the practices Jody has shared in this little book that you, too, will learn to enjoy Christmas, to savor the wonder and experience the joy of this most miraculous of seasons, and to worship anew the One whose birth is, truly, the reason for this season—and for all the others.

K. C. Ireton
Edmonds, Washington
August 2017

Finding the Heart Of Christmas

One virtue of keeping the seasons of the sacral year is that they can help us to redress an imbalance, either in our own spiritual life or in the culture of our church or denomination.

[R]edressing an imbalance ... [can] help us restore that quietness, that inner peace, that willingness to wait unfulfilled in the dark, in the midst of a season that conspires to do nothing but fling bling and tinsel at us right through December.

-Malcolm Guite, Waiting on the Word

For most children, from littles to teens, the Christmas holidays revolve around talking about presents, getting presents and playing with presents. And, for good measure, celebrating with a birthday cake for Jesus, especially if those children get to spend time in church. For the grown-ups, we simply long to be with family and friends, sing our favorite Christmas songs and celebrate Christ's birth either at church or in our homes. Of course, there's the fun of watching the aforementioned children or grandchildren unwrap all those gifts on Christmas morning. For this Nana of five grandchildren and counting, it is one of my greatest joys.

But I'm with Malcolm; it seems like the season "conspires to do nothing but fling bling and tinsel" at me all the way through December. Guite's poetry is some of my favorite; he's British and brilliant and his rich writing makes language come alive. However, as with any treasure trove of richness, sometimes I have to dig deeper—what does "redress" mean, anyway? I discovered the original meaning was "to arrange or set in order again," but in English it now means "to set right" in the sense of "to rectify."

Yes, our Christmas celebrations need to be "set right." The holiday season can run from peaceful moments of humming along to Christmas tunes while drinking your favorite beverage to the all-out craziness of the Christmas morning extravaganza. In between are all the preparations and planning while that quiet voice reminds us what the season is all about—peace, joy, family and Jesus. It can be hard to find a balance with it all.

Parents do their best to manage this tricky equation of dealing with the pressure to provide nonstop happiness and joy for their kids while keeping the heart of Christmas. Most often, though, all that fun and excitement leaves us feeling exhausted and overwhelmed while the joy and peace we crave are lost. I know I've experienced many Christmas mornings where the surroundings mirror my senses: discarded gift wrap, leftover boxes and used-up bows lay in piles on the floor; I feel worn out. *Maybe you can relate.*

Because we are connected beings—body, soul and spirit—when one part of us is out of balance, it affects all the rest. My prayer as you read the following pages of *Living the Season Well* is that you discover a way to "redress that imbalance." Instead of succumbing to a season that wants to "fling bling and tinsel at us right through December," I pray you'll begin the journey of making small changes now that will leave more room in this Christmas season for the joy and peace your family craves.

When someone asks, "Are you all ready for Christmas?" you will have an answer that reflects a subtle shift, a slowing down and a simplifying of the season in a way that gets to the heart of Christmas.

But What If I Don't Have Kids?

For it is good to be children sometimes, and never better than at Christmas, when its mighty Founder was a child himself.

Charles Dickens, *A Christmas Carol*

While I am aware there are different ages, stages and life seasons of my readers—singles, Double Income, No Kids (DINKS), empty nesters—the fact is, Christmas is a holiday that focuses on children. I wrote *Living the Season Well* with my own grandchildren in mind and a secondary audience of aunts, uncles, grandparents and friends of families with children. Perhaps you'll think of nieces or nephews or maybe the kids next door as you read, particularly Chapters 4 and 5. If you keep that in mind, you'll be able to adapt the ideas accordingly.

Perhaps the real significance of Christmas is that we need it so much. Now there are people who say they feel it is purely commercialized, it has lost its real spirit.
But this is not so.

-*Gladys Taber,* Stillmeadow Seasons

Taber wrote *Stillmeadow Seasons* in 1950. She could well support her opinion that the Christmas spirit had not been lost since her observations were written when times were simpler, different and less fractured. I agree wholeheartedly that "the real significance of Christmas is that we need it so much," but the way we keep Christmas in this current decade feels light years away from the celebration it once was. Our annual remembrance of the birth of Christ needs a recalibration, not with the Global Positioning System (GPS) but with our Jesus Positioning System, our JPS.

If you answered "yes" to either question on the back cover of this book—"Does it seem like each December ramps up to the exhausting pinnacle of Christmas Day? Do you feel a keen letdown the day after?"—your response says you're ready to make an adjustment to your Christmas celebrations. You, too, feel the need to get closer to the heart of Christmas—peace and joy, family and Jesus. You long to slow down and simplify your holiday practices, but where do you start? Is there a way to reorient our culture's thinking? Our own?

Yes. We begin by living the season well.

What do I mean by *"living well"*? How about simplifying and savoring the moments instead of rush-rush-rushing to the next thing? As countercultural as it seems, our satisfaction with the season of Christmas might be greatest when we do as close to nothing as we can—leave the activities and shopping and programs and choose to just rest, if not physically then mentally and visually, from all the input and movement. Keep things simple.

When the holiday season is upon us, moms, dads and extended family members spend a great deal of time and effort finding things for their kids to *do*. Children often feel like Christmas is something that happens *to* them rather than something they've experienced. They're hurried to get out the door for a party or program and end up tired or agitated. Fussy outfits for Santa photos make them cross and uncomfortable, while activities not of their choosing show up on the calendar and out the door they go. May I suggest you present your children with choices about what they want to do? Is it Santa photos or not? (Unless Nana is paying for them. Then this is non-negotiable.) Do all the children want to pile into the van and see the Christmas lights? If not, maybe you can hire a babysitter and just you and your loved one go. *Alone.* Enjoy the quiet. And if you have teenagers, even better. Find you favorite drive-through, grab a hot beverage and go.

Simplify, slow down, savor.

Word Play—*The Church Year*

Worldwide history is always referenced by that watershed moment when Christ came to earth. We mark time as either B.C., "Before Christ," or A.D., *Anno Domini*, Latin, meaning "the year of our Lord." It makes sense, then, that we should keep time according to a church calendar, particularly as believers in a kingdom that is not of this world.

The church year or church calendar (used interchangeably) has two parts, like a large circle divided in two. One arc of the circle places the beginning of the church year on the first Sunday of Advent, four Sundays before Christmas. This period stretches until Pentecost in May or June and tells the story of the *life of Christ.* The second arc of the circle goes from Pentecost until Christ the King Sunday at the end of November and tells the story of the *life of the church.*

Living the Season Well is about the arc of those days in the cycle that reach from December through February telling the life of Christ. In the pages ahead, I will weave the church calendar liturgies into Christmas practices for today's families, introducing you to some age-old traditions that have a built-in rhythm making room for the comfort and joy we seek in the season.

While it's true that "Jesus is the reason for the season," as my 7-year-old grandson has often told me, the season is more than just one day. There is a way to widen our worship into *all* the holy days from Advent, beginning

on the fourth Sunday before Christmas all the way
through Epiphany (Jesus' presentation to the Gentiles)
on January 6. Instead of putting all our energy into the
parties, preparations and presents, taking a look at the
traditional practices of the church year can make room
for God's presence. Being intentional about our attention
can bring more of the joy and peace we crave at
Christmas.

As an evangelical churchgoer *Being intentional about our*
with a faith background of over 40 *attention can bring more of*
years, I have only recently begun *the joy and peace we crave at*
to embrace a new way of thinking *Christmas.*
about the Christmas holidays as they are reflected in
the older church liturgies and traditions. When I was
introduced to K.C. Ireton's book *The Circle of Seasons,*
I discovered this "uniquely Christian way of marking
time" that comes via the church calendar, anchoring our
days in a Godward view of life. I'm finding myself drawn
to the rich traditions provided through the liturgies in
the church year that surround the Christmas season and
would love to see an overflow of these new (old) discov-
eries into the lives of my fellow evangelicals.

Word Play—*liturgy, sacral (or We Are Not Afraid of Latin)*

Due in part to my church background, the word *liturgy*
used to conjure up all manner of repetitious and mean-
ingless prayers. Perhaps that has been your perception

as well. I have been surprised to discover that, at its core, *liturgy* means simply "the work of the people" and comes from the Greek word *leitourgia*.

I have been surprised to discover that, at its core, liturgy means simply "the work of the people" and comes from the Greek word, leitourgia.

One of Webster's definitions says liturgy is "a prescribed form of worship." The form and framework of simple, repeated practices make a space for God to show up. That can only be a good thing, right? When liturgy is included in our worship, it is not only beautiful but life-giving because we know the Source of our worship is alive and oh-so-well.

Malcolm Guite's opening quotation also contains the old-fashioned word *sacral*. It may look familiar-ish; it is part of the word family that includes *sacred* or *sacrament*—from the Latin, *sacramentum*, meaning "oath," or *sacrare*, "to consecrate." The sacraments or liturgy surrounding the fasts and feasts of the Christmas season set aside (or consecrate) an action as a way to acknowledge God's presence. A sacrament could be as familiar as your family's meal of clam chowder on Christmas Eve—something you do that acknowledges the time as special and set apart.

A sacrament is as familiar as your family's meal of clam chowder on Christmas Eve; something you do that acknowledges the time as special and set apart.

Sharing a meal, reading Scripture and lighting a candle on these occasions are ways to pause and invite in God's presence.

Applying the Practices

In the pages to come, I'll offer some practical ideas that you can adopt or adapt from the church calendar traditions to use in your own celebrations. You will find no "shoulds" for the season but some new (based on very *old*) practices and simple steps to make more room for joy in a way that works for you and your family.

Ireton's *The Circle of Seasons* was key to my understanding of these liturgies and traditions, and I'll reference it often in the coming pages. Through my reading I've become more familiar with these traditions and am thrilled to be learning how to relish the slowing down these rituals and observances can afford me. If you'd like to know more about the calendar of the entire church year, Ireton's book is a good place to start.

So, What's Inside?

The heart of *Living the Season Well* is not intended to add one more thing to *do*; it is a way to encourage a change of mind and heart about the season of Christmas. Inside, you will find examples and ideas to help slowly change your family celebrations so they will:

- Bring you, your children and extended family closer to God's heart for the season
- Infuse celebrations with simple

The heart of Living the Season Well *is not intended to add one more thing to do; it is a way to encourage a change of mind and heart about the season of Christmas.*

joy and a balanced view of giving and receiving
- Widen Christmas worship beyond one single day
- In particular, you will find suggestions for observing these church calendar fasts and feasts:
- **Advent**—Preparing our hearts with the slow advance of the weeks before Christmas.
- Most of us, particularly children, don't do waiting well, but we're waiting for a Savior, making room. How do we do that? I'll share some ideas that involve reciting Scripture and lighting candles with a nod to those chocolate calendars from YaYa (or whatever term of endearment you have for Grandma).
- **Christmas**—This feast day wasn't always celebrated by the church. That surprised me. How can we own this holiday as Christians, observing it not with "here's what I want" but with "this is what I'd like to give" or "this is how I can help"—a different focus that honors the birth of Christ?
- **The Twelve Days between Christmas and Epiphany**—Tradition calls this period "Twelvetide," a pause built into the church year for a slow unwind and nudge to the other side of the year. The Twelve Days of Christmas is a lot more than just a song.
- **Epiphany**—This church observance ends the Christmas season on January 6. *Epiphany* means *manifestation* or *showing forth,* the celebration of Christ's appearing to the Gentiles represented by the three Magi. Church practices are varied and fun; one includes ushering in a new year by marking the occa-

sion (literally—there's chalk involved!) with a doorway equation and saying a house blessing. *Oh, and there's camel food.*

Living the Season Well is based on my personal interaction with immediate and extended family, particularly my five grandchildren; 20-plus years of classroom experiences with young children; and years of being around kids in Sunday School.

From these experiences, I will speak to the pressures of the season of gift-giving and suggest ways to channel all that Christmas energy and deal with the drama and trauma of expectations (children's and grownups'). I'll also share a few tips on ways to incorporate those always/everywhere screens—phones, tablets and computers—using them as resources and tools.

In these pages, young families will find help in resisting the cultural craziness so the holiday can be reclaimed from the gift-giving, soul-draining frenzy it has become. When I see the pressure of the season weighing on my children and grandchildren or listen to folks in line at the department store complaining about the loss of Christmas cheer, I find it sobering to think we have lost the joy of this season.

So what can be done to turn around this Titanic-sized ship of busyness as we sail through the holidays? We can weave together the life of contemporary families with the liturgies and traditions surrounding Advent, Christmas and Epiphany, and that practice is just what *Living the Season Well* is all about. The ideas you find here will show you a way to make room for reclaiming the heart of joy at the center of Christmas. Who doesn't need more joy?[1]

How to Read this Book

Each chapter of *Living the Season Well* may include one or more of these sections:

- **"History Lesson"** with brief background information surrounding the feasts and fasts of the Christmas season within the church calendar year. (Yes, there are fasts during Christmas. Crazy, huh?)
- **"Word Play"** will unpack new vocabulary, as you've seen demonstrated already.
- **"Learning Opportunities"** provides activity ideas that can be adapted for families who homeschool their children.
- **"Action Ideas"** is where you will find practical tips and ideas to adopt or adapt as your family eases into this new approach for the Christmas season. And the best part? Each of these activities is a low-cost or no-cost opportunity to engage your kids and family in the holiday. Each chapter will include 5 or 6 suggestions that will work for children of all ages.

You will find this book is short-ish and sweet (like a candy cane or a peppermint latte). That is on purpose. I

---

1. NOTE: *Living the Season Well* is not a collection of crafts, activities and recipes to do with your family. Nor is it a daily devotional for the season with inspirational readings or poems. You will find mention of many Christmas resources for grown-ups and children—books, calendars and the like—in the Appendix.

want it to be a Christmas primer of sorts, something portable, easy-to-use and stashable in a purse or bag. Much more on the practical side and not too precious. In fact, you are invited to write in the margins or anywhere else you find an "Aha!" that strikes you. (Please tell me I'm not the only one who reads with a pencil in her hand.)

As you read, may I suggest you consider a question: What family practices do you have for the Christmas season and why? Examine the *heart* of what you do—is there something that can be added or taken away? And if overconsumption is an issue, ask God to show you why or how that has come to be. We know what we spend time and money on is a reflection of our beliefs and what we value. Overextending our time can be just as depleting as overextending our wallets. What's important to you about Christmas? Some prayerful, reflective moments can be very revealing, as can just talking with your spouse or family about what this coming season will look like.

Lest you get the impression that I've mastered this church calendar path and put the brakes on an over-the-top Christmas in my own life, let me be clear. While I want to adopt or adapt the ideas I describe here, I have only made baby steps in our home. Last year I labeled the candles in an Advent wreath on our dining table with the Sunday Watchwords—*Wait, Prepare, Rejoice and Love* (see Chapter 2). The display sparked my husband's interest and prompted a question in a very puzzled voice, "What're those? The fruit of the Spirit? You're like five short." My response provided an opportunity to tell him what I'm learning, about the slowing down of the season with a weekly stop to light an Advent candle. "The watchwords are like an anchor," I told him. "Holding us in a place of reflection if even for the five minutes it takes to read a passage and pray." He was only slightly less puzzled, but it was a start.

Living the Season Well is about learning new habits of the head and the heart, which translate to the work of our hands. So where do we begin? I've briefly mentioned the church calendar (also called the church year) and defined *liturgy* and *sacral* here in our Introduction. Those words may be new to you as they were to me, or maybe they were hiding in the shadows, covered with a little church dust.

Why don't we shake them off and bring them into the light?

CHAPTER 1

A Subtle Shift

UNWRAPPING THE GIFT OF LITURGY

As with much of Christianity, the church year can be radically countercultural, a much-needed light showing a better way to live. In a culture that is often too hurried and distracted, the church year helps us pay attention because it draws our focus continually back to Christ.

—K. C. Ireton, The Circle of Seasons: Meeting God in the Church Year

I think we can all agree that Jesus is the main thing about Christmas. He is God-made-flesh and come to Earth, born as a baby in a manger on that first Christmas morning. For many, thoughts of Jesus as a child lead us to thinking about the children in our own lives, whether they're our children or grandchildren, nieces, nephews or siblings. With the young people in mind, we grown-ups go to great lengths to infuse the Christmas holiday with as much wonder and magic as we can and delight in watching the joy this brings.

When our son and daughter were growing up, we did not raise them with an awareness of the holy days of the church calendar. The denomination we raised them in rarely, if ever, mentioned Advent or Epiphany. Our churches observed Christmas Eve and Christmas in quite honorable fashion with candlelight services on Christmas Eve and the usual kid-filled Christmas pageants, but that was the limit of our Christmas season experience. Outside the walls where we worshipped, the culture's focus and fever-pitched festivities seeped into our practices.

And that fever-pitched focus seeps in still.

To quote the Apostle Paul slightly out of context, "My brethren, these things ought not to be so." As believers in Christ, we can model something different to the world. Our wallets will not provide the way to happiness. Regardless of holiday season messages around us that say, "Do more! Buy more!" we can choose a silent resistance of sorts. As the opening quotation suggests, anchoring our days in the rhythm of the church year reminds us and others, whether in line at the store or talking with our family at home, why we are celebrating the birth of our Savior Jesus.

Fleshing Out Meaning

As mentioned in the introduction, the word "liturgy" comes from the Greek *leitos,* of the people, + *ergon,* work: *leitourgia,* in other words, is "the work of the people" or public duty. It's odd to me that liturgical practices have been looked on with some skepticism in many evangelical churches. As Christians *the work of the people* is when we flesh out our roles as being light in the world and honoring God with our words and practices. And what better time to do that than at Christmas, when a dark world needs this light?

Annual Christmas liturgies are like a glance from a moving train with a view onto the same landscape. The "landscape" is our daily life, and the rituals are the reminders to slow down as we travel, giving us a gift of hope. We revisit familiar terrain each year we "pass by" Christmas in the annual traditions that surround the holiday; thus, the liturgies become an icon through which we see God.[2]

Word Play—*Icon*

The word *icon* is from the Greek word *eikon*, meaning *likeness, image* or *picture*. How icons ended up being a term for the thumbprint graphics on a computer desktop seems a little odd. But think about it. When you click on a particular icon, a way is opened that takes you to view what's inside, a window to another place, and widens your vision to something more. This technological use of the term, embraced by all of us who own a computer, is derived from Orthodox Christian theology, where icons are considered a window into the holy. Each simple

The word icon is from the Greek word eikon, meaning likeness, image or picture.

---

2. "It is not simply that on this occasion we see from a train window, but that as finite beings we only have 'window-minds' … always knowing that what we pass through, and what passes through us, is a partial and incomplete glimpse of something greater than ourselves." M. Guite, from *Waiting on the Word*, notes on Luci Shaw poem for December 5.

outline of a cross or candle or a drawing of the star of Bethlehem is a symbol that helps us catch a glimpse of God. They are a part of the annual liturgies of Christmas.

Revisiting Rituals

Rituals encase memories. They link the past and present. They choreograph the dance of intimacy that families and friends perform. They give us access to one another. Sometimes rituals facilitate growth. Sometimes they express the breaches gaping between us. But always, rituals have power.

-*Wendy Wright,* The Vigil-Keeping Watch in the Season of Christ's Coming

I used to shy away from connecting the word "ritual" with anything in the church. The connotation of the word—so planned and confined—didn't leave much room for the spontaneity of the Spirit of God. But I've found there is great comfort in the repetition of a prayer, a benediction or psalm, one that engages us with other believers. This tradition of prayers lifted around the world throughout time reminds us we are part of something bigger than ourselves. Whether reciting the Doxology or the 23rd Psalm, taking communion or saying the Lord's Prayer in unison, these practices bring us back to the center—where God is.

A ritual is simply a custom or practice of a formal kind—formal in the sense that it has a form, something repeated and defined. When we use a form, it makes space for something. Annual holiday practices, rituals if

you will, can become a means to seeing God more fully.
Simple things like lighting a candle
and reciting Scripture tune us to
the practice of looking for Jesus in
the Christmas season when we
intentionally hold a space for
Him to come.

A ritual is simply a custom or practice of a formal kind—formal in the sense that it has a form, something repeated and defined.

Habits that Change Our Hearts

When our extended family gathers at my brother's house
for our monthly meal, we link hands or elbows in a circle
while everyone puts their right toe down on the kitchen
floor. The practice came from my nieces' ballet classes,
and the movements have morphed their way into our ritual. Various shoeware, from hiking boots to leather flats,
reveals a disparate bunch of folks, all ages, sizes and personalities gathered in that circle to pray. After the "amen,"
we all bend our knees and lift our toes, ballerina-like, placing them back on the well-worn wooden floor; our simple
actions have united us. Although it's more silly than formal, we've repeated this practice for many, many years.
We know when we finish our prayer that God has been
welcomed into our midst, keeping us ever aware that He
will show up in our conversations over the meal to come.

Many of the early church traditions and practices surrounding the Christmas season are like that—an outward
movement that flows inward, encouraging us to tune in
and listen. We become aware of God's presence, welcom-

ing Him into our midst; we are on the lookout for Him to show up. The feasts and fasts in the church calendar become markers that anchor the year, returning us over and over again to the same observances, a way of remembering, calling us to a message of assurance, hope and joy.

Our secular celebrations do that, too, marking the seasons with birthdays, anniversaries, adoption days and the like. We anchor our years, adorning our homes with flags, banners or balloons. Sing a particular song, bake a favorite cake. Whether mindfully quiet or joyously noisy, we are reminded each year to stop for a moment and reflect, re-focus our vision, keeping in mind what matters. These holiday traditions and special occasions anchor our years as we circle through our days.

Easing into the Season

Introducing your family—kids, grandparents and relatives—to the liturgy of the church year, along with adjusting your own practices, could cause some resistance. The word "tradition" seems like another word for "lifeless" or "stuffy" and people will balk. What folks want is a vibrant celebration that will satisfy their souls; they might need a nudge towards this new discovery.

Here's an idea: When you're proposing even a subtle shift from what you've been doing for a very long time, people need some advance warning, right? A little buttering up to soften the blow. I've had decades to practice this; if there's one thing that's saved me all the years I've been married, it's learning how to communicate well. (*Learning* is the operative word.)

Communication Cornerstone—The Preamble (aka The Caveat)

When I get ready to throw a curve ball of an idea my husband's way, I might say something like:

"Honey, I know this is hugely different from what we've been doing for all this time, but I'd like to suggest ..."

Then I launch into my revelation, mentioning where I'd actually like to go on vacation this year (instead of visiting the in-laws) or how I totally changed my mind about the kind of car I think we should get. By communicating my awareness that this is a completely new idea, I help him come prepared to the new suggestion. You can do the same for your family.

The changes I'm suggesting in this book about living the season well might be less than cataclysmic. Perhaps you will see them more as a refinement to your family's particular practices. However, for those of you to whom I'm suggesting an entirely new way of marking the season of Christ's birth, the ideas in these pages might create nothing short of a mutiny. It might be a quiet and peaceful mutiny, but people might threaten to jump overboard nonetheless.

When your family cries, "We're gonna do what?!" my prayer is you'll stay the course, and while I make no guarantees, you may be less stressed this Christmas season if you adopt or adapt some of these ideas. Our children and grandchildren mimic what they hear and model what we do. When we model peace and joy, slowing down the season, we help them adjust their perspective about Christmas.

Our children and grandchildren mimic what they hear and model what we do.

If you embark on this sea change of thinking, you may be surprised at what you see change.

You might find that you, your children and extended family members are happier, and (not to go all Michael Jackson on you) the world will be a better place.

The Good News at the End of this Book

If these church calendar observances are as new to you as they were for me and, frankly, Just Too Much Right Now, you can consider this first read as a learning season; next year, you'll be better prepared. However, if you want to make some simple changes *now*, there are some empty pages at the end of the book just perfect for writing down your ideas.

As my brother the pastor once said, unknowingly launching the idea for this book into the world—

Start small. Start now.

CHAPTER 2

Advent

WHY WAITING MATTERS

M oving a family of four across two states in the dead of winter is not for the faint of heart. When we sold our house in October, the closing date took longer than expected, leaving us moving smack in the middle of the Christmas season. The kids' Christmas vacation from school was all the time we had—a two-week break was the perfect window. Well, maybe perfect isn't exactly the right word. Looking back, it was rather a bold move, but I was determined to be near family again, and Seattle was calling.

We had spent 12 rich years in our central California neighborhood, woven deeply into the community. Our daughter and son, 12 and 15, had attended school with the same group of friends all their short lives. We were firmly ensconced in the life of our church as well as a babysitting co-op whose members had become like family. School, church and community were tightly woven into our lives.

During the weeks of preparation for our move, I frantically pondered how we were going to keep Christmas as we were uprooted and on the road during the holidays. My practical husband was in a very focused Task Mode. However, plucking my children (and myself) away from our life-giving support system had *me* focused on our emotional needs. My son Aaron and I share a similar temperament—both of us people persons, super adaptable and outgoing. He would be fine. Our daughter, however, was at that awkward, in-between stage of adolescence. Leah had two bosom friends she'd known almost from birth, and they meant the world to her. Moving her in the middle of sixth grade didn't help; I needed a way to ease her (well, all of us) through the coming transition, so I hatched a plan.

Crazy-Making Long Distance Christmas Plans

My husband and I began communicating with my brother and sister-in-law, the family to whom we would finally be close, and commissioned them with finding us a home to rent before we committed to purchasing a new one. Securing a temporary place to live was the biggest piece of the puzzle but filling that home with Christmas holiday presence was going to be the next hurdle. Many phone calls and not a few letters were exchanged in the weeks before we left, and we were miraculously able to find a temporary home.

Then I asked my brother for one more favor: Could they manage to have a Christmas tree up when we arrived? And maybe some lights? I think I sent them $20. When we finally left our home in Central California and headed towards the Pacific Northwest, the anxious feeling in my stomach grew with every mile. How was our family going to adapt in this season? What had we done? And what about Christmas?

Our trip lasted well into the second evening of travel when we arrived at my brother's house in frigid pouring rain. We stumbled into bed and woke the next morning with excitement and uncertainty about our new home. I secretly wondered whether Alex and Pam had been able to pull off the Christmas tree and lights surprise. "After all," I thought, "they've had six weeks to prepare."

A group of volunteers from my brother's church showed up after breakfast to lead the way to our new home. We drove across town and up a winding hilly street through a middle-class neighborhood, stopping in front of a house painted a rather noncommittal color of mustard, something between yellow and gold. The rain continued to pour as we trundled out of the rented truck's cab.

Pam ran ahead to the front steps. "Wait, wait!" she hollered. "I need to run in and get things ready." I smiled a secret smile—maybe they'd been able to pull off this Christmas surprise after all.

She reappeared in the doorway and beckoned us. "Close your eyes!" We were led up three front steps, through the door and into the living room. I smelled cinnamon and heard Christmas carols in the background.

"Open your eyes!" There in front of us was a simply adorned Christmas tree with red paper bows and strings of popcorn. There were indeed little twinkle lights sparkling on the tree, a fragrant pot of cinnamon potpourri simmering in the kitchen and Christmas songs playing on a small tape player. I burst into tears and stood there speechless.

"How did you ...?" I stammered. My husband and children stood dumbfounded.

There was a huddle of arms and hugs while more tears flowed.

"Merry Christmas," my brother breathed gently. "Welcome home."

That was twenty-five years ago. I still have the red bows.

Jesus is Coming—Make Room

Waiting to celebrate the birth of Christ can be like that move—a slow preparing of our hearts, our minds and our homes, like the planning I undertook with my brother and sister-in-law weeks before our Christmas in a foreign land. Besides the planning and waiting, I had to give up many expectations of what Christmas would be like that year. How do you celebrate the holiday when your living room is crowded with moving boxes? But the good news? Surrendering my ideas of perfection left space for God to surprise us beyond what we could imagine. I was forced to adjust to a new season as

I looked at all the extra room and vacant corners in our new rental.

The empty walls and barely furnished rooms greatly improved my mental state, making it easier to "see." Although I felt untethered and impatient, desperate to begin nesting in our new home, the emptiness created room for waiting. Life is funny like that. Whether it's clearing our calendars for an hour or cleaning out an overstuffed closet, getting rid of our "too much" leaves space for relishing and enjoying what's to come. Or allows us to see what's already there.

Whether it's clearing our calendars for an hour or cleaning out an overstuffed closet, getting rid of our "too much" leaves space for relishing and enjoying what's to come.

The focus and intent of the Advent season provide just that: space to wait—physically, spiritually and mentally—to prepare ourselves for Christ's arrival, His birth. These weeks before Christmas can also provide the necessary period of time to adjust our expectations about the Christmas holidays, which can be fraught with high and low emotions.

History Lesson *and* Word Play—*Advent*

In the Western church, Advent begins on the fourth Sunday before Christmas. Advent is the beginning of the church year and anchors the season of Christmas. Most consumer-driven Advent calendars start on December 1, but the actual first day of Advent is different and changes every year. Because of this, the length of the Advent season changes annually as well. A Google search will reveal the first day of Advent; in 2018 it's December 2nd.

The word *advent* comes from the Latin *adventus,* which means *arrival* or *to come. Adventus* is similar to the Greek word *parousia,* which means *a being near* and is commonly used to refer to the Second Coming of Christ. While we celebrate Advent to mark the occasion of Christ's first coming, it is also an occasion to recall that He is coming again.

The word advent comes from the Latin adventus, which means arrival or to come.

Advent was also originally a period of fasting in preparation for the feast of the Nativity (now Christmas), which was practiced in some form as early as 400 A.D. Unfortunately for us, Advent as a season of fasting and reflection has all but disappeared from many evangelical church landscapes. (More about fasting in the next chapter). Advent has been defined, instead, as the number of shopping/party/activity days there are until Christmas. In all our busyness, we may be making a list and checking it twice, physically and materially preparing for Christmas, but we seldom stop long enough to ponder the meaning of Christ's coming into our world.

Consider this comparison. Two to three mornings a week I stop to exercise on my stationary bike. All I can think about is when I'll be finished. (What a wimp!) I know the back-and-forth, up-and-down movement is good for me, but while I'm cycling and huffing, the only thing on my mind is what's next in my day.

So I pass the time, maybe five whole minutes, by

counting "one-one-thousand, two-one-thousand, three-one-thousand" while I pump my arms. I want to get the blood flowing to my tight, achy muscles, and I'm depending on the oxygen that courses through my heart to give me the desired result. I may be improving blood flow, but I end up tense instead of relaxed; I'm too busy reciting "one-one-thousand, two-one-thousand" in my head. Rather than breathe into the stretches with my body, my mind takes over, ticking off the seconds.

*One hundred and twenty-one thousands l*ater I realize what I'm doing. Ack. Talk about counterproductive. Finally, I pay attention to the beating of my heart, loosen my grip and concentrate on breathing slowly and deeply in and out. I'm painfully aware of how seldom I stop to breathe deeply, and I vow to make an improvement in that area. There is a sure-fire benefit to my body when I do this; it's a benefit to my soul as well.

Instead of ticking off the days until Christmas, making the smallest, simplest changes during the season can have positive results in helping us slow down and savor the moments. Just five minutes of quiet in the morning, evening or middle of the day, with or without a child on your lap, can make a difference.

Practice inhaling and exhaling slowly. Remember that the Holy Spirit, the *pneuma* or breath of God, is our source of life. Counting down the days rather than making the days count will leave you in a place of tension rather than peace. Instead, look for chances to steal those moments of stillness. Go for a walk, raining, snowing or clear. Look out the window for three minutes and notice the sky, the light, the shadows. Stop and breathe deep into the season of Christmas and resist the pull that wants to stretch you out in all the worst ways. This is making the days and moments count.

Wait Training

So, what do we *do* in those four weeks before our Christmas celebration? If we have "eternity set in our hearts," as Ecclesiastes 3:11 says, how can we live with lingering? The Hebrew word *qavah*, translated as *wait* in Psalm 130:5, can also be translated "hope." The Hebrew meaning is *gather together, tarry* or *look eagerly for.*

Theologian Henri Nouwen has called the season of Advent a time of "active waiting," a mix of patience and anticipation of what's to come.

Nouwen says, "Active waiting means to be present fully to the moment, in the conviction that something is happening where you are and that you want to be present to it."[3] *Wait training* helps us attend to the heart and soul, the reason for the Christmas season—Christ's first coming.

The weekly watchwords of Advent will help: *Wait, Prepare, Rejoice and Love.*

---

3. *The Circle of Seasons-Meeting God in the Church Year*, K.C. Ireton, p. 23.

Action Ideas—*Advent Wreath*

The ritual surrounding Advent wreaths is simple—light a candle and read from Scripture on each of the four Sundays before Christmas. An Advent wreath isn't a "wreath" in the regular sense of the word, but a round tabletop candleholder with four places for candles. (I found mine at Goodwill.) The circular shape reminds us that the Christmas season is only one point along the way in the cycle of days where we live. By marking the four Sundays of Advent with the weekly candles—surrounded by greenery, if you'd like—we stretch out the anticipation and provide ourselves the needed space to slow down.

Church tradition tells us the candle colors for an Advent wreath consist of one pink candle and three purple candles. There also may be one candle in the middle, white or gold, which is the Christ candle and remains unlit until Christmas Eve. Each week your family can formally observe this waiting season by lighting a candle and repeating the traditional words of Advent, taken from the 15th Chapter of John.

Candlelighter: *"Jesus Christ is the light of the world."*

Everyone else: *"The light no darkness overcomes."*

This weekly practice also involves Scripture reading that includes verses about a biblical person identified with that day. The week's candle is lit and someone reads the Bible verse associated with

Candlelighter: "Jesus Christ is the light of the world." Everyone else: "The light no darkness overcomes."

that week. Your kids can take turns with candle lighting and, if they are able, reading the Bible passage. These are the candle colors and watchwords for Advent[4]:

Color	Day	Watchword	Person/Text
Purple	First Sunday	*WAIT*	Isaiah (Isaiah 9:6&7, Micah 5:2, 7:7)
Purple	Second Sunday	*PREPARE*	John the Baptist (Mark 1:2&3)
Pink	Third Sunday	*REJOICE*	Mary (Luke 1:46–49)
Purple	Fourth Sunday	*LOVE*	Jesus (I John 4:7–9)
White/Gold	Christmas	*EMMANUEL*	Jesus' Birth (John 12:46, Luke 1:78&79)

May I suggest you don't *have* to use pink and purple candles if you use an Advent wreath? Remember, the saying is "adopt or adapt." Yes, the liturgical colors are symbolic and important—purple for repentance, pink for joy, white for purity—but the point is not the color. The point is to remind yourself each week that Jesus is the light of the world. (And frankly, pink and purple make me think of pastel Easter eggs. Different holiday.)

If all you have is red, green or gold candles, use those.

---

4. As a #CluelessEvangelical who is new to this practice, I've adapted the traditional Scriptures to reflect those I thought fit the day better. You may discover through your own experience or in other sources that these are different.

If the white candles were on sale, use those. Make your own "wreath" by setting four candles in a circle on a tray with the Christ candle in the middle. Use what you have and do what works for you. *The point is to slow down and remember.*

The point is to slow down and remember.

About Lighting All those Candles

I was maybe 8 years old when my mother taught me to light a match. I remember the grown-up feeling I used to get when she would ask me to light one of her cigarettes. (*I know, I know.*) The raspy scratch of sulphur across flinty paper and the sudden "Whoosh!" as it flamed up always gave me a little thrill.

Each family is different, and you know your children or grandchildren best, but I would like to suggest you consider showing them how to use matches. (More fires have been started by kids *playing* with matches than by those who knew what they were doing.) What gift of accomplishment might you hand your 8-, 9- or 10-year-old when you teach them how to safely strike a match and light a candle? After the four weeks of Advent practice and recitation, I'll bet each time a candle is lit, no matter what occasion, the words will rush back to them: "Jesus Christ is the Light of the world, the light which no darkness overcomes."

The key to learning is repetition with variation, which is why God made Sunday School.[5] The same lessons year

---

5. The phrase "repetition with variation" was coined by Jean Piaget in reference to educating young children. Piaget was a Swiss clinical psychologist known for his pioneering work in child development.

after year come wrapped in a different way, helping children remember. The practice of lighting a candle and reciting a variation on certain words each week has a way of sinking in gradually and staying there so that we can remember, too. Slowing down, being still, reflecting on the season is a lesson we all need.

But Grandma Already Bought Us an Advent Calendar

If you've decided to light candles each week during Advent, what do you do with the calendar you bought or were given—the one with 24 days of chocolate? Or 24 days of Lego figures (that would be my daughter and son-in-law) counting down the days until Christmas morning and all those presents? While the novelty of an Advent calendar is an attraction for young and old—"Ooooh, what's behind today's picture? Let's find out!"—the focus is still on something at the end: Christmas Day—yippee! Presents. Candy. *No sleep.*

And what if you get behind a few days in the process and find the 16th, 17th and 18th all crashing into each other? You know what I mean—the days are long, you're busy at work, the afterhours find you cramming in all the extra preparations for the season. It's hard to stop the hamster wheel and take even 10 extra minutes for all the fanfare accompanying "What's behind door number 12?" when your life is maxed out with caring for kids, managing homework and getting dinner on the table.

The Advent wreath is a nice alternative to the daily

Advent calendar. It's a simple weekly, not daily, ceremony that can provide the pause you and your family need to recalibrate. Lighting the candles is a Sunday occasion; life is usually slower on Sundays ... usually. Also, the beauty of an Advent wreath is that it's made in a circle, reminding us that life goes on after Jesus is born, and we cycle through the days post-Christmas and into the New Year.

But go ahead and hang up the Advent calendar anyway. Nana will be thrilled.

Start small. Start now.

CHAPTER 3

Getting Ready

PREPARING OUR HOMES, HEADS AND HEARTS

One year when I was teaching full-time, I was that mom trying to cover all her bases *and* take care of Christmas. I adjusted my expectations and asked my college-age daughter and her friend to decorate for the season. This process involved them lugging two enormous boxes up the stairs from the garage, unpacking the decorations with care and exercising their newfound power as home decorators. I said a lot of quiet prayers. *I hope they put the three snowmen together the way they're supposed to. And my mother's glass angel; please, God, don't let it break.*

This passing of the decorating mantle involved tremendous trust on my part. I left the house that morning at 7:30 and headed out to wrangle second-graders while I pondered the transformation (or disaster?) I might behold that afternoon upon my return.

Leah and her friend Lisette did not disappoint. A snapshot from that afternoon testifies to their success. Lisette is wearing ornaments as earrings, and Leah has a big gold bow hugging her brown locks. They had some fun while completing their task, and although things were not arranged the way I would have done them, the house looked perfect.

As you and your family are preparing your hearts and minds for Christmas, you are no doubt preparing your home. Everyone's styles and tastes are different. Some people have themes—Birds! Stars! Snowmen! Angels!—and others simply put their favorite things out wherever they like. "Theme? There is no theme." (That would be me.)

Creating an invisible environment of peace and joy at Christmas time is often directly connected to the physical environment and how concerned we are about it. If everything has to look like a Macy's store display or be Pinterest-perfect, you may be setting yourself up for not only extra stress but disappointment as well. So how do we dial it down to de-pressurize our Christmas preparations? Here are some low-cost/no-cost suggestions.

Action Ideas—*Decorating*

What about having your children help you? (Or maybe you already do.) Even the young ones can help in some small way. Perhaps less can be more this year.

1. Instead of purchasing greenery from the store, choose some greens from your yard (or your mom's yard) and bring them in for your mantel or windowsills. In the South, it could be magnolia branches. In the Pacific Northwest, we use evergreen boughs.

2. Have your children make red and green paper chains

and tape them up on the wall and windows. Add to the ones they brought home from school. *Buy more tape.*

3. Set up the Nativity scene, *very carefully.* Talk about the figures and who's in the display.

   - Leave baby Jesus out of the manger until Christmas Eve. Have one child be the "babysitter" for the season. (Buy a backup baby Jesus, just in case.)

   - Put the Wise Men (Magi) way back in another room and move them each day (or week) a little closer to the scene. After all, the Magi didn't come to see Jesus at least until Epiphany on January 6, two weeks later. Or maybe it was two years. (You may need to buy some backup Wise Men, too, in case their overseer loses them.)

4. Are you sending out Christmas cards or a Christmas letter? Good for you! Have your children help stuff cards in envelopes and add the address labels. Talk about the recipients as you go. Pray for them.

5. "We're sending electronic cards. It's midnight, and my kids are in bed."

   - Okay. How about giving your teenager the task of choosing the photos (as a reward for doing his or her homework)?

   - Or letting them choose the card design (ditto on the homework).

Some Thoughts on Christmas Trees

One year, when my friend Holly was moving during Christmas time (another adventurous soul), it didn't make sense for her to purchase a Christmas tree since all the ornaments had been packed away for weeks. Instead, she set up a ladder in her front room, a fitting addition to the family while their lives were in transition. She draped the ladder with Christmas lights and texted me the photo because she knew I'd get a kick out of it. Now, when I come across the picture in my phone or my Instagram feed, it reminds me to be a little more chill about what the perfect Christmas "tree" should be.

When my son and his wife were first married, they couldn't afford a tree, so they devised their own by stringing green strands of mini-lights up on the wall in a fir-tree shape. Christmas tree—done.

Maybe this year you don't have to hunt for a fresh tree from the U-Cut lot to adorn the family room unless you like lying on the ground in the mud, freezing cold, while holding a hacksaw in your frozen hands (or asking your Significant Other to volunteer).

Perhaps you can get your lovely fir down at the local hardware store, and when you've got it set up in the designated corner (after cutting off the trunk two or three times to balance it in the tree stand doo-wah), simply drape it with lights.[6] Add the ornaments a little at a time—*there's*

---

6. "Thingamajig," "whatchamacallit." Our family likes "doo-wah."

an Advent practice—and keep some in the boxes. You don't have to unpack Every. Single. One.

Or you could abandon yourself to the spirit of adventure and wait until Christmas Eve to get your tree, inviting the family to decorate with you. The advantage here is that you can leave it up longer—maybe until January 6, Epiphany—and when you dismantle everything, the branches won't be quite as crunchy and brown.

Or you could buy an artificial tree. (Heresy? Maybe, but not messy.)

Christmas Season Expectations

Adjusting our Christmas season reality involves not only dialing back on decorations (or not), what kind of tree we get (and when), but also the challenge to simplify our gift-giving if we want to adjust the overconsumption gauge. The easiest (or perhaps not) and most important way to change the pressure cooker of Christmas season expectations begins with the grown-ups. We adults set the pace for Christmas peace.

We adults set the pace for Christmas peace.

Yes, it starts when we embrace the idea of bringing balance—all the change flows from there. Truth is, putting the "Merry" in Christmas is often wound up in our own identity, an identity that comes from providing children with a magical Christmas, the just-right holiday experience. This is a big burden to carry and we have to take the risk to do less. Although it is a risk, it can bear much fruit in the lives of our children. Fruit like peace and contentment and joy.

Talking It Out

Countless tears have been shed by families near and far on Christmas morning. Sometimes there are no tears, just very hurt feelings and the unspoken weight of misunderstanding. Why this crestfallen display of emotion? Because our Christmas expectations often don't line up with reality, no matter how hard we try to make things perfect.

"I thought you would ..." "I didn't get what I want ..." "Didn't Grandma read my list?"

Grown-ups and children alike have spoken and unspoken wish lists, often with accompanying cut-outs from the Sunday newspaper ads or print outs from their Amazon wish list. Grown-ups sometimes have the greatest challenge here; it's those often unspoken wishes that cause the most hurt when they are not fulfilled. I have some personal experience with this, being Ms. Intuitive married to Mr. Concrete Thinker. I expect my sweet husband to read my mind every Christmas about what I'm pining for. After all, I've been dropping all kinds of subtle hints. Poor man.

Every family is different. There is no one-size-fits-all solution for working out the particulars of giving and receiving presents at Christmas, especially when the bottom line is finances. Discuss expectations with family members, immediate and extended. Have practical conversations about money with your children (more about that in the Chapter 5). Have some philosophical conversations with relatives about your goals to keep the focus less on presents and more on making room for God's presence. Your family, especially grandparents and in-laws, may tune you out and ignore your desires, but you've said your piece. And since our children mimic what we say, when they overhear these conversations it might prompt a change in their thinking, too.

Start small. Start now.

Fasting—Giving Up to Make Room

Fast, therefore, until His Passion brings the world home free. He works through any crosses He can find. In a time of affluence, fasting may well be the simplest one of all.

—Robert Farrar Capon, The Supper of the Lamb

For busy families with active children and full schedules, simplifying decorations for house and home and dialing down the focus on presents can be helpful in making more "Godspace" in your life, to use a term from blogger Christine Sine. Now we'll look at another preparation of the heart—our appetites. The word *appetite* conjures up a picture of food, but we know some "foods" feed not just our body but our souls and spirits as well.

Did you know that each morning when you serve a bowl of oatmeal or pop a Pop-Tart for your children, you are breaking your fast from the night before? This is why we call the first meal of the day "breakfast." Even your first cup of coffee or tea qualifies. *Why, yes, this IS my breakfast.*

The practice of fasting seems like a shocking suggestion prior to the rich celebration of Christmas. But it makes sense when you think about it. Letting go of, putting off or making room for one thing makes space for something else. When we take baby steps towards dealing with our desires (the "flesh"), we become tuned in our spirits to hear God and give Him room to speak.

Fasting during Advent can simply be a variation of giving up, putting off, setting aside or laying down to ultimately provide a way to make room for Jesus in our hearts, mind and spirits, where we are hungriest. Jesus said in John 6 that He is the bread of life. It is no coincidence that He was born in Bethlehem—the House of Bread.

One of the best reasons for fasting during Christmas season is because there are so many other things that want to "feed" us. Too much of anything can fill me so full that I never know I'm hungry. The Christmas season provides the greatest number of opportunities to drive this lesson home. Thousands of sparkly doodads, an overabundance of rich food, an explosion of visual input from every possible screen in the universe—how many Christmas specials can there be? Seriously.

Too much of anything can fill me so full that I never know I'm hungry.

It is possible to cut back, fasting from all that input. Physical hunger can turn us towards feeding our spirits instead of our flesh; limiting visual overstuffing via all manner of social media can also do the same as we look to be fed from the Bread of Life.

History Lesson—*Fasting*

The practice of fasting before Christmas was instituted by Bishop Perpetuus of Tours in the fourth century. He ordered fasting three days a week from the day after St. Martin's Day (November 11) until Christmas Day. In the sixth century, local councils encouraged fasting on *all* days except Saturdays and Sundays from St. Martin's Day to Epiphany on January 6. This period of fasting was later shortened and simply called "Advent" by the church as the practice was widely accepted.

But what about life in the 21st century? How can we adapt or adjust the practice in a way that will add to our lives in the right now where we live? Especially in the *now* that is Christmas?

Nature (and people) abhor a vacuum. If you take one thing away, something comes in to take its place. If you decide to fast from food during the Christmas season, "denying your flesh," as the Apostle Paul reminds us, your spiritual hunger awareness grows. Ask God to fill that space, with more love or patience or kindness. Be aware of listening for God's voice as He speaks in the gaps.

Be aware of listening for God's voice as He speaks in the gaps.

So, what can you fast from during this season? It doesn't have to be food. How about these options?

Action Ideas—*Fast from all that Visual "Noise"*

Turn off your screens—phones, tablets, computers—for

60 to 90 minutes and relish the freedom that quiet brings. Of course, it may be noisy now that you've got time to read one more book to your kids. But that's a good kind of noise, the kind that feeds the soul—theirs and yours. Having your children also limit their visual media input is another way for them to fast. You might say, "Sometimes there's noise we hear and sometimes there's noise we see. All that makes it hard to hear and see God. Mom and Dad are going to spend less time with their phone/computer/tablet during Advent. When would you like to give up some of your screen time?" This phrasing frames the question in a way that communicates they *will* cut back, but it also gives them the power to choose how and when.

I'm not talking about stopping all visual media, but cutting back, taking baby steps to help children adjust their thinking, too. You could also say, "Do you want to limit your game time on Mom's phone during the car ride home from school or while we're at the grocery store?" "Do you want to give up your tablet during quiet time or before bed?"

You get the idea.

Fast from the "Shoulds"

Take a break from certain visual media channels that keep you focused on "everybody else." Facebook's siren song or Pinterest and Instagram come to mind—whatever social vortex seems to suck you in during the holidays. These platforms can be helpful for creativity but can also be a rabbit hole of, "Oooohhh, I should make *this*. No, I should try *this. Everybody else is." Maybe.* Lay it down. Turn it off. Put it away. And ask God to show you what can be done with what you already have.

Fasting from Food

If you have children, of course they'll need their three squares a day. The practice of fasting from food when it comes to children is clearly fraught with questions. Should they participate? Will they even understand what they're doing? What's the point?

The point, to repeat a theme here, is to adopt or adapt older practices of Advent in a way that makes sense today. Consider this. If our children get everything they want whenever they want it, we all know this is not a good thing. One way to help children understand they cannot always have whatever they want is to practice even a simple fast. Marcie, a mom I know, explained it like this:

"The kids have never done it, but when I fasted for [our Bible study], I explained it as giving up something that makes you feel comfortable and satisfied so you can get those feelings from God instead. And to put yourself in a place where you need to ask God for help to get through a tough situation instead of relying on yourself or other things."

What about fasting from certain foods with your kids, saving your enjoyment for Christmas when you will break your fast together? Perhaps meats (ham, beef, whatever), sweets or a particular treat. Or you could set aside Sundays, traditionally the "feast days" on the church calendar, as days to look forward to those special foods. (Chocolate totally counts as a special food.)

I'm not suggesting anything radical here but more of a subtle shift in thinking about the way we look at Christmas with all its too-much. Consider taking out all the fake food that promises to feed our soul and replacing it with holy nutrition.

Honoring, adopting or adapting some of the traditions of Advent is a great way to do that.

Start small. Start now.

CHAPTER 4

What About the Presents?

CHANGING THE WAY WE GIVE

L ike fasting from sweets, meats or screens, if we're going to cut back on something that impacts our body, soul or spirit, we need something else to fill it. Suggesting we curtail or change up our Christmas present practices (pun intended) can be an equivalent shock to the system, for children as well as grown-ups. There's not much I need these days in the way of gifts, but I know I'd be disappointed if my husband and kids didn't mark Christmas Day with some kind of heartfelt surprise.

Christmas Presents or God's Presence?

Exchanging gifts during the Christmas season seems to be a given for most everyone. Whether it's cornhusk dolls, homemade crafts, the latest TV or a talking doll, people have been giving and receiving presents for hundreds of years. The custom of gift-giving at Christmas comes from the example of the Wise Men who brought gifts to Jesus as told in the Gospel of Matthew, Chapter 2. We honor Jesus and each other by expressing our love with our gifts.

One way to live well in the Christmas season begins with adjusting the focus on gifts. We can take that desire to show our love and bless others by teaching our children (and ourselves) that it's better to give than receive. But how do we do that? If Christmas is too commercialized, as we are wont to lament, is there anything we can do in response? Exchanging presents is a good thing, clearly a God thing. But it is not the only thing about Christmas.

Let me be clear; I don't want to sound like a Grinch in this discussion of giving and receiving. My husband and I have showered each other with surprises for many, many Christmases. And like many of you, I spent numerous holiday seasons looking for that just-right gift. Whether it was staying up until all hours searching Amazon for the correct *Inside/Out* Disney characters for my grandkids or doing a similar search for my daughter when she was little (then, the search involved Toys 'R' Us and Cabbage Patch dolls), *I can relate*. And my son was forever asking for Legos (as his sons do today). We bought a lot of Legos.

Finding the Balance

Whether it's Legos, the latest electronics or a mess of little cars, the focus at Christmas is often all about the presents. We've said children model our actions and mimic our words. During the Christmas season, they will be looking to the grownups to see how we translate the holiday into our lives. Are we "go and do and buy" or "slow and simple, *Are we "go and do and buy" or "slow and simple, let's ask why"?*

let's ask why"? Or somewhere in between? We can model thoughtful choices that reflect the heart of God's gift to us as we enter this power-packed time of year. It takes intentionality, but we can help the children we know—nephews, nieces or our own kids—balance the pressures of wanting more than they need while missing what they already have.

Our desires to have a particular so-and-so in order to be happy can be met with joy in the receiving, but we can also come up feeling empty when said gift doesn't fill the longing we have. Children know this desperate feeling and need the most help understanding and identifying the gap. It is an indicator that we are spiritual beings made for a relationship with Jesus, whose birth we are celebrating, and that we were made to be with each other. One way to keep Jesus at the center of Christmas is by reminding everyone that we reason we celebrate is to honor Jesus and be with family.

So how do we lean into that Jesus-at-the-center awareness, translating this truth into our lives during a season that wants to throw us into a gift-giving frenzy at every turn? The world around us yells loudly through glittering advertisements, constant music and television specials, day and night, shouting, "*This* is what Christmas is all about." "This will make you happy." It's hard to hear the truth for all the noise.

With some intentionality and purpose, we can reverse that cultural chaos that talks about all we have to have right now. We can turn down the noise. We can make efforts towards establishing more peace and joy and simplifying our Christmas celebrations by adjusting our view about giving and receiving presents.

This issue is really one of balance—living the season well so you and your family aren't overwhelmed. *The overwhelm can begin with the barometer of our bank balance, so why don't we start there?*

Balancing the Budget

Depending on the ages of kids in your family and how much you want to divulge, one way to begin the Christmas gift discussion is by thinking about how much money you have for gifts. Extend the conversation to the relatives as well, if you can. (Talking about money can be tricky; I advise praying about it first.) Christmas budgets can be tough, but if you've been setting aside a little each month (we waited waaaaay too long to begin that practice), you will have a head start, even if it's $20 each month.

If you have little ones at home, fashion a way to say this in code: "Papa works very hard, and his money goes to help us live, so we have to be very wise about how we spend what we have," or something like that. Talk about how everything you have comes from the hand of God, even if Dad or Mom are the ones working. Most kids under the age of 15 know that one or both of their parents work but have no idea there are actual spending limits for things like Christmas. You'll figure it out.

For teenagers, I say give them the cold hard facts. You could say, "Mom and/or Dad (or both) make _____ each month to support our family. The Xbox or Nike shoes you want cost _____, so let's look at the *whole* Christmas giving picture. The one with everybody in it."

Giving as a Family

When you begin the Christmas gifts discussion, open the conversation by proposing your family give something first.

When you begin the Christmas gifts discussion, open the conversation by proposing your family *give* something first. Not to each other but to a cause you can trust and believe in, one that will do good work with the funds you have. Go through the process of deciding how much you can give. It could be a small monthly gift to a nonprofit you want to support, but the point is you're still other-focused first. (There is a list in the Appendix of trustworthy causes I have personally given to or know about.)

Giving your time is also a precious gift. After a day serving in a soup kitchen or local mission, there might be a subtle change of heart about your family's Christmas desires next year. Investigate where you can volunteer to serve others at Christmas and engage your teenagers in the process by asking them to do the research. Today's reality is such that every other child you see, regardless of age, has a phone or tablet in their hands or nearby. So how can we take advantage of this everywhere visual, online presence during the Christmas season? Make those electronics part of the occasion.

When I taught middle school, I found that seventh and

eighth graders had enough ideas and energy to save the world if I could figure out how to channel it. Kids this age can be some of the greatest advocates for other-centered causes and care if they are given the chance. We live in a screen-filled world; use this to your benefit and turn your teenager loose with your family's budget in mind (within reason, of course). Let them research the best place to give—maybe they have a cause they're passionate about. When young people are engaged in the giving process, their hearts are invested in the practice.

And the practice is giving.

When young people are engaged in the giving process, their hearts are invested in the practice.

Parents can also model this other-centered giving easily. When your spouse or loved ones ask, "What do you want for Christmas?" consider mentioning one item you'd like and then tell them about a special cause you'd like to give to, asking them to make a donation in your name. Jesus' words remind us that He is all about loving others *as we love ourselves*. Self-care—especially during the holidays—is important. But sacrificing what we want to help others also models what love looks like in a balanced way.

When Budgets are Tight

I know what it's like to be without the means to provide Christmas gifts for your family. When our children were very young, my husband was unemployed for eight long months. We received some food stamp assistance and lived on unemployment during that time, but when it came to the holidays, we had zero money for Christmas. Although our small home group knew our needs because we shared life with them weekly, we didn't specifically ask for help at Christmas. But God is always keeping watch over us.

Come Christmas week, imagine our surprise to hear a honk outside our front door, run to open it and discover boxes of gifts in all manner of holiday wrapping on the front porch. There was a doll for my daughter and trucks for my son, clothes for each of them, plus handmade tree ornaments for our family. I recall a honey-baked ham was included along with some instant tea and Tang mixed together; the 1980s were alive and well.

Many families live close to the bone these days, no matter how heroic their efforts to budget. Here are some ways to engage your family in the process if you are faced with financial challenges this Christmas.

Action Ideas—*Giving and Getting*

Teach your kids to pray about the financial situation in your home, whether you have a little or a lot

- Teach your kids to pray about the financial situation in your home, whether you have a little or a lot. Model for them the confidence that God sees your family's need and will never leave you alone, that He longs to surprise and bless you and others through you
- Check in with relatives who may be able to help with your children's wish lists. Aunts, uncles, grandmas and grandpas are great about that.

- Stretch the budget by shopping at small, local thrift stores.[7]
- Your school secretary may also know of local non-profits that want to help families like yours if finances are tight.

Turn your kids' attention to what they can give without money being spent. Maybe write a thoughtful, encouraging note to a neighbor or draw a picture and send that along to the recipient. Bake something and take the treat to a friend or neighbor who might need a thoughtful and caring touch at Christmas time. As a retired educator, I can tell you this is a surefire way to bless a teacher; some of my most memorable gifts received during my teaching career were handmade or homemade.

Action Ideas—*Christmas Creativity*

Here are some more family activities and experiences that cost little financially but convey God's other-centered focus for the Christmas season. They also provide an opportunity to channel all that gift-centered energy.

- Do you have a go-getter elementary-aged kiddo? Perhaps he or she can organize a kid-centric gift drive for a family at school. Have your children's teacher check with the school secretaries; they're an invaluable resource for this. They know many family details about kids that attend the school and will

---

7. In our extended family, we call them "gettin' places." "I love that necklace. Where'd you get it?" "At the gettin' place."

probably know where there's a need.

- Your church is also a place where there are needs at Christmas. Ask your pastor or a staff member if there's a family you can help, even if it's something as simple as a visit to deliver home-made cookies. Hearts and hands together go a long way during the holidays.

Hearts and hands together go a long way during the holidays

- Have some outgoing, creative tweens at your house? Maybe they could canvass the neighbors and invite them to participate in a Christmas lighting contest for the neighborhood (even if the neighborhood is apartment balconies).

- Your family can play Secret Santa and adopt a new-to-the-neighborhood family nearby. Even if they don't celebrate Christmas, you can bake some cookies, leave them on the doorstep with a handwritten note and sneak away. Encourage your kids to use their imagination *and all that energy.*

We've talked about gift ideas for families. Now let's look at the kids.

Pre-Schoolers

As a grandmother, I can tell you nothing means more to me than receiving something in the mail from my grandkids. Here is something simple to do with your youngest ones that costs nothing but time and effort.

Letter Writing—Instead of writing letters to Santa Claus (well, you scribe the letters and they scribble their name), have your littles write a letter to an out-of-town relative—aunt, uncle, cousin, grandparent—or maybe to their favorite teacher. It doesn't have to be an actual "letter" per se; it could simply be drawings from their little hands with your added captions.

While they're working, talk about how God sent his "letter" to us—the Bible—and how Jesus is God's gift to us. Since we have Jesus, we have something to give away to others—our love. Then mail the letters (or hand-deliver them in person when they aren't looking).

Since we have Jesus, we have something to give away to others—our love.

Give Two First—The young ones in the family have no doubt been telling parents, grandparents and extended family what they want for Christmas since it was their birthday, like last June. Here's a thought to help foster concern for others while thinking of themselves (the way Jesus would): When they're talking about what they want for Christmas, have them choose two toys to give away *first*. Decide with them which agency you'd like to support with your donations. Decorate a paper grocery bag and put in the books and toys, games or puzzles (no, probably not puzzles. Too many loose pieces) that they've decided to give away. Then deliver the box or bags together as a family.

Creative Wish Lists—When the gift requests are coming fast and furious, direct your youngest to the Sunday newspaper ads or weekly sales flyers. (You might need to enlist an older sibling to help.) Have them cut out pictures of what they want (set a limit) and glue them to a piece of paper. Stuff them in a junk mail envelope (recycling!) then "mail" to the powers that be, i.e. Santa, Mom, Dad or grandparents. Tell those who can write to jot down their ideas but set gift limits. Boundaries make you choose what's important.

Boundaries make you choose what's important.

Elementary School Age

Writing again. (Sorry—this retired teacher can't help herself.) Okay, so many kids aren't as comfortable writing as they are with desktops, laptops or tablets.

Encourage your school-age child to share with their teacher or a relative via typing (a.k.a. hunt and peck) what they're doing for the Christmas season. For example, "Our family decided to change our focus this year from receiving gifts to giving, so we're giving to [name your charity], which I think is really cool." Or "Our family wants to remember what the Christmas season is about sharing God's love, and I want you to know I care about you" or a similar heartfelt sentiment. Print out the message and send it along.

Learning Opportunity—*This is a perfect time to teach kids how to address a letter.*

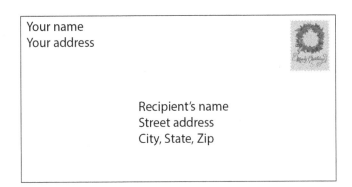

You're welcome.

If you have an 8- to 10-year-old boy who swoons over Marvel comics, Ninja Turtles or Justice League superheroes and communicating is not going to happen, this may be a stretch, but the mantra is "adopt or adapt," right?

About those Wish Lists

I still have my son Aaron's Christmas list from third grade. He included his sister and organized the requests into a Venn diagram—"Things I Want," "Things Leah Wants," "Things We Both Want." *Who says you can't use math in everyday life?* I also have another year's list on butcher paper that is nearly as long as my kids were tall. Yes, there is no end to what your kids will want for Christmas.

Suggest that school-agers join their younger siblings in choosing two toys *in complete working order* to give away for every one that they want. Task the older kids with the process of finding somewhere to donate their possessions. Goodwill is an option, but there may be an agency in town that helps new moms or struggling families; talk about sharing with them. Model what this process looks like by delivering the bag to the Goodwill or Salvation Army truck next time you get groceries. Talk about how God has blessed you with abundance so you'll have some to give away. Check with your pastor or church staff and see if there is a family who could benefit from some gently used toys.

Have a conversation with your children about the desires we have for things to make us happy when this desire was meant to be filled by God. Explain that our wants or desires are not bad things, not at all—there's a reason I love the color red and you like lavender. We all have gifts and interests that are in our God-given DNA. *God delights* in seeing some of our Christmas dreams fulfilled, especially if it means receiving a 98-color paint set or that One Special Something that we've longed for.

Make God's love and HIS creativity part of the Christmas gift conversation and part of your kids' prayers. Consider a discussion of the Apostle Paul's words in II Corinthians: "So we fix our eyes not on what is seen, but on what is unseen, since what is seen is temporary, but what is unseen is eternal" (4:18). What does that mean to you as a parent? What does that mean to your kids? My friend Nancy shares Matthew 6:19-21, updated for kids: "Don't count on even your best toy-treasures to make you completely and forever happy. Toys get old; toys break. God made us; he knows best what will make us truly happy."

What do these verses mean for Christmas? There are some great table talk ideas right there.

Tweens and Teens

When I first became a Twitter convert, I was flummoxed about how I could say something within the 140-character limit (which has since been upped to 280). What does social media have to do with Christmas? The limitation proved a great way to be creative. It bears repeating: Boundaries make you choose what's important. Whether your budget is bottomless or not, having limits is a good thing as it can lead to all kinds of original solutions.

If you've discussed the Christmas budget with your kids, let your teens run the numbers for what they want. Their thoughts might go like this: *Here's my Christmas list. Here's what this stuff costs.* As they begin to research online, use the Sunday ads, or window-shop the stores; perhaps a revelation will occur. *Oh wow, I should probably do some babysitting or dogwalking. I need more money for that iPhone, iPad, or Xbox. Then I can wrap it and put it under the tree myself.* Your children will learn more about God's faithfulness when they have some skin in the game of Christmas shopping and celebrations.

NOTE: If your teenagers or your family use Amazon for online shopping, look at the features of Amazon Smile.

Purchases made via this portal go through their foundation which donates 0.5% of the price of eligible purchases to the charitable organizations selected by customers.[8]

One Final Thought

Regardless of how the Christmas gift message is conveyed—whether kids text you photos of what they want, cut out Sunday ads and make a collage or write a good old-fashioned list or letter—encourage them to pray while they wait. Whether you or "Santa" (aka Mom, Dad and/ or relatives) answers their prayers for gifts, this focus on prayer turns their attention to God as the source. Not to say that God will give us all we ask for, including a Star Wars Lego set, but God is the ultimate provider of all we have, whether it's a little or a lot.

Lighting the weekly Advent candles on the Sundays before Christmas is a way we keep watch and wait, looking for our Savior to come. Leaving our lists in the hands of someone else while we wait for Christmas morning can be part of that waiting, too. Which brings us around to where we began—the ultimate Christmas gift is Jesus. If we keep the spirit of who He is at the center of our celebrations, we will indeed be *living the season well.*

Start small. Start now.

---

8. My .5% (every little bit helps!) goes to REST Ministries here in Seattle. More information about their work is in the Appendix.

CHAPTER 5

Christmas

SAVORING THE CELEBRATION

Midnight on December 24 is the hinge between Advent and Christmas, the door that opens and moves us from waiting to celebrating. In spite of all the noise in the rest of the world—Christmas songs everywhere we go, TV specials and holiday movies, advertising jingles for all manner of gifts—we often find an hour of quiet on Christmas Eve. If we have observed the church calendar practices of Advent, waiting through the weeks of December with expectation, our hearts are tuned to this turning point. We are ready to receive our King.

Now, we light the Christ candle—gold or white—and read the passage from Luke 1:26-38 that foretells the birth of Christ. We share the reading with family at home or as part of our church's Christmas Eve service. While I've never been adventurous enough to attend a midnight service on Christmas Eve, our family has attended many services in the early evening hours. It is one of my favorite times all year to be in church. And since my children live in other cities, it is also the rare time of year when we all get to be together.

People are packed in the sanctuary shoulder to shoulder, eyes trained on the stage in front. Baby Jesus has been laid in the manger. The congregation settles in to listen to a short message. We lift our voices in songs and carols, and then the pastor invites us to begin lighting the tapers we've held in our hands or stashed under our chairs.

One by one, the flames are passed from those along the center aisle toward those at the edges as, in a whisper, neighbor declares to neighbor, "Jesus Christ is the light of the world." Sanctuary lights are dimmed, and even the youngest children are hushed by the silence. When the last candle is lit, our worship pastor begins strumming "Silent Night," and we raise our voices together, accompanied only by the acoustic guitar. It is near impossible to sing the words for all the tears in my eyes and the catch in my throat.

Every year I think, "Never mind Christmas morning. Never mind the presents. My Christmas celebration is complete." Then I remember the children and their Christmas Eve thoughts; visions of sugarplums and Santa Claus fill their precious heads. Of course, all the parents can think about is sleep.

I recall one Christmas Eve when my son and his wife stayed overnight with us so we could all be together when our two young grandsons woke up the next morning. We tucked the kids into bed that night after church and proceeded to turn our living room into Santa's workshop. I don't recall exactly what my son and daughter-in-law were building, but I'm pretty sure it was something from that big box store that begins with the letter "I." There was a wagon to assemble as well, red planks and black wheels piled on the carpet. Our favorite Mannheim Steamroller Christmas CD was playing while we drank eggnog and noshed on Christmas cookies and sugared pecans. I was focused on filling up Christmas stockings, and my husband was tasked with rummaging through the party decorations.

"See if you can find the *Happy Birthday* banner," I told him. "Then draw some block letters with J E S U S on them. After you cut them out, tack them up on the end of the banner; we'll have a *Happy Birthday Jesus!* sign."

I handed him a stack of 3 x 5 colored index cards, and he got to work. This project kept him occupied and away from the flotsam and jetsam in the living room. He hates flotsam and jetsam.

A little after midnight the assembly tasks were near completion. It had been a long day and an even longer night. We were giddy from sleeplessness, nearing the twilight zone (you know what I mean), and we still weren't finished. My husband suddenly exclaimed, "Look! I finished it!"

Tacked up on our dining room wall above the table, this proclamation proudly displayed, "Happy Birthday Jseus."

"Honey, it says, 'Happy Birthday Jay Seuss.'" (I now have a coffee mug to commemorate the evening.)

Hubby was bleary-eyed and hadn't even noticed. My son and his wife burst into laughter, then tears while we joined them. I'm so thankful I snapped a photo before my husband took it down and reversed the letters.

J E S U S. Happy Birthday, Jesus.

Yes, we know whose birthday it is, but the fact is *we* get all the presents. Weaving together the wonder of Christmas involves one part birth of our Savior and one part life of a saint. Nicholas, to be exact. It would be easy to blame our culture and their cashing in, literally, on the character of Santa Claus, but let's not be so hasty. You might be surprised to learn the real story of St. Nick.

St. Nicholas Was a Real Swell Guy

The character of Santa Claus is based on the life of an actual person, St. Nicholas of Myra, from a village in modern Turkey.

The character of Santa Claus is based on the life of an actual person, St. Nicholas of Myra, from a village in modern Turkey. The church calendar recognizes his generous life with the feast day of St. Nicholas on December 6. And no wonder; He was a generous man as well as a champion of the poor, employing people to make clothing for the needy and distributing food to the hungry. One of the best-known stories about him provides a toehold on the origin of Christmas stockings. (Sorry.)

Nicholas had a friend, a wealthy shipping merchant, who lost all of his ships and their cargo during a violent storm. The man was devastated because he had three daughters of marrying age and with this loss went any chance of contributing wealth to their dowries. Nicholas wanted to help. He had the resources, but he knew his friend would hesitate to take charity. Nicholas came up with a plan; after dark one night, he dropped a bag of gold coins through the open window of the eldest daughter's room. Some of the coins fell into a stocking that had been hung out to dry. His generous act became the tradition we have hundreds of years later of hanging those stockings "by the chimney with care."[9]

If your family celebrates the birth of Jesus as the central focus of Christmas, bringing Santa into the mix can be sticky business. Some families deal with that mix in a stellar way. One family I know observes the church feast day of St. Nicholas as the day they open their family stockings. You may consider doing this, using it not only as an opportunity to tell your children about the real St. Nick but also to spread out the bounty of Christmas morning to more than a single day.

When I posed the Santa question on social media, my friend Marcie responded, "We do full-out Santa. Make lists, leave the fireplace doors open so he can get in the house, cookies and milk, carrots for the reindeer. The biggest and best present is left until Christmas Eve and it's from Santa. Childhood is so fleeting, I'm going to eke out every bit of magic I can before my kids are too old to believe anymore."

"Christmas," she continued, "is absolutely the day we celebrate Jesus and his birthday. My kids have never ques-

---

9. Adapted from an entry in my *World Book Encyclopedia*, 1954, origins of St. Nicholas. Yes, I still have encyclopedias on my shelf.

tioned why Santa exists on Jesus' birthday. It's two completely separate things in their minds."

I also asked my daughter, now 37, what she remembered about Santa growing up.

"Mom, I don't think you and Dad ever fully explained Santa to us. We knew of course the reason for the season, but I think you left Aaron and me to our own imaginations as far as who Santa was. There was always something magical about the possibility of him really existing and coming down our chimney to our house. However, I do remember one Christmas you and Dad were up really early setting up presents and we had to stay in our rooms 'til they were ready but come Christmas morning we always knew it was about Jesus."

I'm not sure about our Christmas parenting gap regarding Santa, but I'm grateful my children felt some kind of magic and mystery about Christmas morning. Like Marcie said, kids grow up way too fast.

Children are smarter than we give them credit for, but they are also very invested in make-believe; their pretend worlds are part of their reality until age 7 or 8. You know your children best and will be able to figure out the balance of truth-telling and make-believe that works for your family.

One caution—there is clearly nothing "spiritual" or not in a family's decision to celebrate Christmas with Santa Claus in the midst.

One caution—there is clearly nothing "spiritual" or not in a family's decision to celebrate Christmas with Santa Claus in the midst. If this has been an issue for you and your family and you have wondered about what to do, consider embracing the spirit of giving that St. Nicholas' life embodied and tell your kids why you include him. The character of Santa Claus is based on the life of a real person who showed us what sacrifice and Christlike giving looked like.

History Lesson—*The Origins of Christmas Day*

You know, Nana, Jesus wasn't really born in December.
—Grandson Paul Silas, age 7

While scholars cannot pinpoint when Christ was born, *we know that He was*. Thanks to good old *World Book Encyclopedia*, we have some background of the Christmas holiday. The origin of the word "Christmas" is a recognition of the Old English "Christes Masse," the three church masses held on Christmas Day in the Middle Ages. For several centuries, Christmas was celebrated as a religious holiday only, and on the church calendar, the Feast of the Nativity was originally celebrated on December 25. It was a way to commemorate the arrival of God's light that countered the darkness in the world.

Although it is not known exactly why December 25 became a cultural day of celebrating Christmas, some factors may have influenced the choice. In A.D. 354 Bishop Liberius of Rome *ordered* the people to celebrate Christmas on December 25. Most likely this date was chosen because the Romans already observed this date as the feast of Saturn, the birthday of the Sun. Perhaps there were some Christians serving in the bishop's palace who encouraged him to choose the day to celebrate the birth of God's Son.

Perhaps there were some Christians serving in the bishop's palace who encouraged him to choose the day to celebrate the birth of God's Son.

Over time, more and more customs were added to the Christmas observances that weren't connected to the church. In fact, during the Middle Ages, these celebrations became so rowdy that Puritans actually banned Christmas in England in 1643.

Those Puritans.

Christmas was later restored by law in 1660. *Thank goodness.*

In the early 19th century, Christmas celebrations were further revived by a movement in the Anglican Church. Charles Dickens and other writers helped in this revival of the holiday. As Geoffrey Rowell has noted, "Dickens' *A Christmas Carol* both reflected and contributed to the Victorian revival of Christmas" by "changing consciousness of Christmas and the way in which it was celebrated" as they emphasized family, religion, gift-giving and social reconciliation.[10]

Thank you, Anglican Church.

Thank you, Charles Dickens. (There's a wonderful Charles Dickens book listed in the Appendix.)

Regardless of the season or the actual day, we know God sent Jesus into the world the first time and that He

---

10. http://www.historytoday.com/geoffrey-rowell/dickens-and-construction-christmas. Accessed 8/15/17.

will come again. That is a reason to rejoice. What better time to celebrate the light of the world than during the long, dark days of December?

The Light Has Come

So, it's Christmas morning and the celebration can begin—Jesus' birthday is finally here!

If your family has used an Advent wreath during the weeks preceding Christmas (and you weren't up at midnight to light it), this is the morning to light the Christ candle in the center. The liturgical color of Christmas is white, symbolizing Christ's purity, or gold, signifying His kingship. As you and your family awaken to Christmas morning, ask someone to light the candle and lead you in the words from Advent: "Jesus Christ is the light of the world," to which others respond, "the light no darkness can overcome." Turn on the Christmas lights and gather around while someone reads the Christmas story from Luke, Chapter 2. Keep your coffee handy and do your best to keep the kids from shaking those boxes and untying those bows. (Unless, of course, they've already snuck in ahead of you; some things never change.)

Tell the kids to move the camels and Wise Men out towards your Nativity scene. (Did you hide them somewhere? Oh, I hope you find them!) We know from the biblical account that the Magi came after Christ's birth, so perhaps they can, along with the camels, inch their way closer to the crèche each day. And tell whoever was in charge of baby Jesus to go find Him and put Him in the manger. (You bought a backup, right?)

Yes, Christmas is here. We've come to the rich celebration for which we've waited. The weeks of Advent were focused on prayer, fasting and repentance; now, it's time to rejoice. Emmanuel, God is with us. In the early days of the church, Christmas did not end when midnight struck on December 25. In more liturgical churches even today, Christmas is a season of the year, with twelve days of feasting until Epiphany on January 6.

Each time you light the Christ candle in the days between now and Epiphany (known as Twelvetide), you will be reminded that indeed the light has come. God is with us. It is time to rejoice. Christmas is more than a day; in fact, it's just begun.

CHAPTER 6

The 12 Days

SPREADING OUT THE HOLIDAY ENERGY

Last year, I told my family I'd like a record player for Christmas. I didn't have two toys to give away in place of the one I wanted, but I did have a couple hundred record albums. I gave none of them away—Keith Green, Second Chapter of Acts, early Joan Baez and James Taylor, all collector's items. Although our current stereo system has a perfectly good turntable, I wanted a phonograph—the portable kind—to play some of the older records, scratches and all. It would be easy to move from one place to another; I particularly wanted to share the experience with my grandchildren so they could see it up close.

"Where does the sound come out, Nana? From that little needle?"

I couldn't wait to show the grandkids a *Sesame Street* album my children played over and over again when they were little, *Christmas Eve on Sesame Street*. Big Bird is on the cover, his tall, yellow, feathery self slumped against a brick wall high on a rooftop in the city. He's plopped down in snow and appears to be half asleep, waiting for Santa Claus. My daughter Leah remembers the song lyrics to this day, having sung "Keep Christmas with You" many, many times as an 8-year-old.

Have you ever wondered if that's possible, to "keep Christmas with you"? When I've found myself enjoying a moment of peace in between the noise of Christmas, I often wonder too: *Why can't this feeling of joy and contentment last all year long?*

I don't think we mean that the shower of presents, the Christmas Muzak or the abundance of sweets and fruitcake should last all year. (Definitely not the fruitcake.)

When we sigh about wanting "Christmas every day," we're really saying we long for peace and joy to last throughout the year.

When we sigh about wanting "Christmas every day," we're really saying we long for peace and joy to last throughout the year. We wish that people would be friendly, not just during the Christmas season but the rest of the year, too. We long to see folks practicing grace and kindness year-round the way Jesus would; we know in our "knower" that is the meaning of Christmas.

History Lesson—*The Twelve Days of Christmas*[11]

Centuries ago the observance and celebration of Christ's birth spanned the 12 days from Christmas to Epiphany on January 6, a 12-day period called "Christmastide"

_____

11. If Christmas Day is the first of the 12 days, then Twelfth Night would be on **January 5**, the eve of Epiphany. If **December 26**, the day after Christmas, is the first day, then Twelfth Night falls on **January 6**, the evening of Epiphany itself.

or "Twelvetide." Hence, the *Twelve Days of Christmas*. Who knew?

On the church calendar, the 12 days are a slow walk from Christmas Day towards Epiphany and end with the feast that observes the appearance of the Magi at the site of the Christ Child. But as our culture often does, veering away from the sacred and turning towards the fun, those 12 days are marked predominantly by a popular rhyme and song more than anything else. "The Twelve Days of Christmas" is sung during the Christmas season, ironically, not during the 12 days it represents.

But 12 Days? Really?

I have two friends who are complete opposites when it comes to ideas about extending the season of Christmas. See which one you relate to.

Nancy's with the *Sesame Street* gang and gauges time by how many days there are until Christmas. Yes, it's her favorite season and, as she told me, "It can't come soon enough." She even keeps a Santa pillow on her bed all year.

Michelle, on the other hand, is so over it. Her Facebook status last December went something like this: "You guys, I couldn't do it. I know it's the 12 days of Christmas, but I caved on day 5. I had to have clean, uncluttered spaces again. Hear me exhaling? I feel like I can breathe! But hey, usually I take down my Christmas decorations on the 26th (one particularly Grinchy year I un-Christmased late on the night of the 25th! Egad!), so progress, right?"

Maybe, like Michelle, you think stretching out the days between Christmas and Epiphany is more like stretching out the stress. It's the day after Christmas, and you are done with celebrating, done with gifting, and you're ready to move on to the year ahead. Your kids might even feel the same—they're back to their old favorite books, puzzles and games, and the high point from all that happiness of new presents has dimmed a bit.

But consider the built-in wisdom afforded by Twelvetide—a centuries-old practice is desperately needed today when we want to over-accelerate our lives. Grown-ups and children can all use some help readjusting. Although most of us do notice the difference between Christmas morning and the days after, children feel it more keenly. Their anticipation is gone, often replaced with a neediness they can't define. And no wonder—when your happy/busy meter has been on HIGH for all those pre-Christmas weeks, the letdown can be terrific.

After Christmas Day, it's time for many children to return to school, revert to a schedule and get to bed on time. That's a difficult transition for kids and parents (although the grownups could be happy-dancing on the sly).

We can't keep Christmas with us *all* year, but maybe a gradual return to normalcy could help alleviate the sudden crash. A slow journey through Twelvetide can allow the time to process both the joy of the gifts and the challenges of the holiday. These 12 days are heading towards

We can't keep Christmas with us all year, but maybe a gradual return to normalcy could help alleviate the sudden crash.

Epiphany, the last feast in the arc of holy days, the sending point of Christmas, *not* the ending.

Action Ideas—*Spread out the Giving*

One family I know spreads out their gift-giving over the 12 days. For a large family like my son's with their five children, that would be unwieldy as well as unwise. But what about devoting one day to each child? People might think you're crazy (well, your kids might think you're crazy). But remember—living the season well means adopting or adapting practices to slow down and simplify the rush and crush of Christmas.

1. Try this: Everyone opens only two gifts on Christmas morning. Oh, the suspense! *Which ones will I choose? The big one? The little one? The shiny one?* Then over the next 12 days, spread it out so Sally and Sam and Sue take turns on those days. (Mom and Dad, you'll have to fit yourselves in.)

2. I also read of a practice where families see how many times they can reuse wrapping paper as they space out their gift-giving—saving the planet and providing some fun. Another advantage of 12 days of gifts? Shopping those post-Christmas sales. Maybe you'll discover that uber-expensive gift on Johnny's wish list is now affordable.

3. We want to focus on Christ more than presents, reminding ourselves of God's presence. What about a

religious-themed ornament, maybe not 12 of them, but four, unwrapping one every third day? One for each child or one for each family member or ... well, get creative. If your Christmas tree is still up, hang them. If the decorations are almost all put away, stow and save them for next year.

But Our Family Always Celebrates on Christmas Day

If your parents, grandparents or siblings plan an annual Christmas Day bash, observing 12 days of gift-giving probably won't work, especially if you have a younger family with newborns or toddlers. And what about the teenagers unwrapping their favorite electronic wonder? There's some anticipation there, too. Half the joy of Christmas morning is seeing it reflected in the faces of loved ones opening gifts; I get that. Grandmas and grandpas, aunts and uncles, have all been looking forward to Christmas Day for weeks, and it would be a shame to disappoint them.

If you want to make an adjustment in your Christmas gift exchange, you will always have the option of changing the days in a way that works best for your family, even in tiny ways. One idea, if you're gathering for Christmas Day with extended family, is to let the kids open all their gifts from the relatives and save the presents from Mom and Dad (or Santa) to spread out over the next 11 days.

The change may be as simple as discussing it over coffee and cake during a less stressful time. Talk about slowing down the season of Christmas and how you and your family would like to focus on a more simple Christmas this year. Adopt or adapt the ideas, even if it's just some soul-pondering for now. It's bound to be a conversation-starter and may open the door to changes for next year.

A Nudge to the Other Side of Christmas

We started the journey into Christmas with the slow weeks of Advent, traveling through Christmas Day, and now we're in the 12 days afterwards, heading towards Epiphany. We can gradually end the season, reminding ourselves once again that Christ's birth is only a resting point along the way around the arc of holy days that heads into the year to come.

Spreading out the energy of Christmas over these 12 days can be as simple as starting a dialogue with your kids where you unpack their thoughts while you pack up the decorations. Conversations with your kids or grandkids while you work can be therapeutic (and helpful) for everyone involved. When hands are busy, hearts and souls relax more easily, providing a chance to process the past weeks. Words like, "I'm sad Christmas is over," "I'm glad Christmas is over," and "What was your favorite part of Christmas?" can all be part of what is shared.

When hands are busy, hearts and souls relax more easily, providing a chance to process the past weeks.

Refresh and recall is the best way to save the memories

of the holiday—the happy, the sad and the in between. The truth is that sometimes there are tears and disappointments during this time of year as well. Here are some ways to keep your hands busy while your hearts unfold.

Action Ideas—*Packing Up*

Consider taking down the decorations and greenery (or brownery) over time. If a self-imposed deadline is needed (getting back to work or school, for example), go for it. Or give yourself all 12 days, if possible.

1. **Ornaments and Decorations**
   Enlist your children to help you put things away. (You had them help put it all out, right?) Decorations may be scattered throughout your home; have them retrieve the unbreakables. Entrust a teenager to unwind the Christmas lights from the tree or help you with undecorating. Older kids can hand you the fragile ornaments, rewrapping as needed, and place them in the boxes. Not all tree decorations are delicate, so invite the little ones to help, too.

   Much in the same way that reviewing Christmas cards calls up memories of friends and family, Christmas ornaments carry their own stories. Maybe your children don't know the glass ornaments belonged to your mom or grandma. What about "Baby's First Christmas"—which baby and who gave it to you? There are many opportunities for talking and sharing here whether your kids hang around for 10 minutes or an hour (miraculous!). Participating as a family in this slow unwind can be a chance for a gradual return to normal after all the hype and activity of Christmas.

2. **Put away the Christmas cards together**
   Place your holiday cards in a basket on the table at dinnertime. Have your youngest pick out the ones they like best—snowmen, polar bears, Santa Claus. As a family, review the names of who they're from: "Who is Aunt Miriam again?" Take turns praying for the folks whose names are on the card. My friend Shanna suggested a variation—save all the photo Christmas cards to use as prayer cards throughout the year. Take turns praying for a different family each month.
   Learning Opportunities
   - Have someone make a list of the names on the cards—alphabetize them!
   - Have each child choose a family and write a note or draw a picture for them—send in the mail.
   - The cards you're not going to keep? Recycle for craft projects—gift tags, bookmarks, repurposed Christmas cards for next year.

3. **Dismantling the Christmas Tree**
   Ornaments are down and packed away, decorations returned to their boxes or tubs. Now it's time for the tree. Do you have a spruce or a fir or something else alive (well, dead, or mostly dead) to dispose of? We used to haul ours out to the deck and down our back stairs, drag it across the lawn and toss it down the

greenbelt, leaving it at the mercy of Mother Nature. Whatever your process, consider enlisting your muscle-bound teens or tweens.

Or maybe you have an artificial tree that has to go back into the box. Several years ago, after considering the perennial needle drop and water filling and, "Can you turn it a little more this way so the empty spot doesn't show?" we finally relented and bought a faux tree. Best Christmas decision ever. But oh my gosh, bending back all those wires and smushing the top on before the handles go back into the sides of the cardboard—it's a Herculean effort. Gather previously mentioned muscle-bound teens or tweens. See if they're game for solving your puzzle.

Remember, these are just suggestions for engaging your family while you extend the days of Christmastide, giving them something to do over the 12 days before the next Church feast day of Epiphany. It's an odd coupling of tasks, true, that combine manual labor with a mind to engaging the spirit, but it may be just the conduit needed for the slow re-entry into the coming new year.

Christmas Dreams

We began this chapter with a nod towards "keeping Christmas with us" all through the year. It's difficult in the days afterward to keep that holiday dream alive: the sense of peace, even fleeting; the warmth and joy we felt being with family. Even if you're ready for the turning over of a new leaf—out with the old, in with the new—we long to carry God's presence with us into whatever we do.

Maybe your dreams and reality collide with each other during the holidays; I know mine do. I'd still like to live in the times of Charles Dickens—waltzing through a Victorian Christmas, drinking eggnog and wassail; watching boys with hoops and sticks while they play their outside games on country roads; dancing at parties in voluminous silken skirts on Christmas Eve.

But isn't that where we sometimes live? Maybe not in Victorian times (who wants all those voluminous skirts or shirts with a million buttons?), but we do have dreams of what Christmas could look like, those visions we carry inside and long to see manifest in our homes, our families and our communities.

My husband and I live on a paved city lane in a Seattle suburb thousands of miles away from any fairy-tale Dickens scene. So, my Christmas reality is very simple—to have my children and grandchildren around a table large enough to seat all 11 of us, a fire crackling in the fireplace and happy conversation. Those are the Christmas gifts that mean the most to me.

But the dream of simpler holiday times prods us all. When we're buried in the commercialism of Christmas, our souls know it's not supposed to be like this. But our "this" can't change overnight. The heart and soul of living the season well is the want-to, the desire for slowing down and simplifying the season. Changing our minds is the first step. Thoughts become actions over time, and time is a gift we all have.

Choose whether you'll adopt or adapt some of these slowing-down ideas during the 12 in-between days of Christmas and Epiphany. Or maybe you'll ponder them for next year, when you can begin again and think about your own dreams for the Christmas season.

Thoughts become actions over time, and time is a gift we all have.

Start small. Start now.

CHAPTER 7

Epiphany

TELLING THE WORLD

When our first grandchild was born, it felt like time stood still for a day. As the words announcing Hanan's birth sounded in our ears, I felt a mixture of astonishment, excitement and awe. The day we'd been looking forward to was finally here; we couldn't drive downtown fast enough. When we finally arrived at the Seattle hospital, I burst into tears of relief and joy at the sight of my still-recovering daughter-in-law and her strapping baby boy.

Giving birth to my own children was miracle enough but standing with my son while he held *his* infant son was more than I could contain. I thought my heart might burst with happiness. Then again, I wasn't the one taking him home. There were no sleep-deprived nights in my future, just expectant thoughts of watching this little one grow.

That little one is nearly 16 years old now and has three brothers and a sister. But he will always be the firstborn who changed our lives.

Of course, a baby's birth affects all the people whose lives it touches. My son and his wife had to make overnight adjustments as their world was trundled and rocked, throwing them into new roles as father and mother. They lost sleep, worried about Hanan's care and puzzled through exactly what it meant to take on this new identity as parents.

As news of a child's arrival into the world ripples onto different shores, it carries a new modifier with it. We refer to the event ever after with, "In the year that Baby ____ was born." In much the same way, the birth of Christ impacts our lives; we live now in *Anno Domini*—the Year of Our Lord.

In much the same way, the birth of Christ impacts our lives; we live now in Anno Domini—the Year of Our Lord.

In the Year that Jesus Was Born

When the Magi came to see Jesus, the event changed not only their lives but all of history. Gospel accounts record that the Jewish parents were visited by these revered men from a faraway land who followed the King's star in the East all the way to Bethlehem. Their visit confirmed a startling announcement, the appearance of Christ to the Gentiles. (More on that in a few paragraphs).

It is worth pausing to consider this festival occasion. Observing Epiphany can become another way to change the focus of Christmas from a single day of gift-giving to what really is The Big Deal—God came to Earth. Just as I often reference time by the year in which I became a grandmother, Christ's birth has become the reference point for all of history. My life has been changed remarkably by both the birth of Christ *and* the birth of my first grandchild.

When we consider the celebration of Christmas and ponder its importance as a season, not just a day, Epiphany on January 6 is the place where the arc of the holidays comes to a slow finish. If we follow the church calendar (there it is again!) we are next ushered into Ordinary Time ("ordinary" from the word "ordinal," meaning counted) as the days progress into a new year and the coming season of spring. Although the January days may look like creation is fast asleep, we are often still moving along at breakneck speed, going and doing. Christmas may be over, but the frenetic holiday pace seems to have picked right up again. Back to school, back to work, back to life.

However, we have a choice about whether or not we continue the countercultural actions of slowing life down, reminding ourselves of the built-in rhythms of God's calendar and His time. Epiphany is a chance to do that by embracing a slower walk through this post-Christmas season as we reflect on the impact of the birth of Jesus.

History Lesson *and* Word Play—*Epiphany*

The word *Epiphany* comes from the Greek and means *manifestation* or *showing forth*. The event marks the visit recorded in Matthew 2 of the Magi, who came to see the King whose star rose in the East—Jesus. Christ's first appearance to the world was to his

The word Epiphany comes from the Greek and means manifestation or showing forth.

Jewish parents at his birth. Epiphany marks his appearance to the Gentiles—in other words, to the rest of the world.

In the early centuries of the church, Epiphany was one of the three major Christian feasts, along with Easter and Pentecost. Originally, both Christ's birth and his baptism were observed on Epiphany and celebrated on January 6. Another name for the observance was "Little Christmas"; some Christians call it "Three Kings Day." In the Eastern Church, this holiday is called Theophany, meaning *divine manifestation*. This Orthodox observance considers Theophany an illustration of the Trinity: Christ himself, the voice of His Heavenly Father and the Holy Spirit in the form of a dove were all present at Jesus' baptism. There are many churches today that observe January 6 this way.

My friend Arielle told me that she and her Eastern Orthodox family celebrate Theophany on January 6. "It is a feast that technically surpasses Christmas in importance and is older in practice to our church traditions," she said. Their priest says particular blessings over homes in the neighborhood, and there is a special service at church. Arielle is also one of the stalwart folks who wait to take down Christmas decorations and the tree that day. "My dream is to hold a big winter bonfire with the tree and all the Christmas greenery, but I'm too nervous to do that in our Portland neighborhood!" she said. *They could roast a lot of marshmallows.*

In the fourth century, Jesus' birth gradually became separated from his baptism (now observed on the Sunday following Epiphany), and Epiphany instead became associated with the visit of the Magi and the appearance of Christ to the Gentiles. Portraying the Magi as kings was a result of the early Christians' reading of Isaiah Chapter 60:

1. *Arise, shine; for your light has come, And the glory of the Lord has risen upon you.*
3. *Nations will come to your light, And kings to the brightness of your rising.*
6. *A multitude of camels will cover you, The young camels of Midian and Ephah; All those from Sheba will come; They will bring gold and frankincense, And will bear good news of the praises of the Lord.*

In the eighth century, an English church historian, the Venerable Bede, recorded some "embellishments" of Matthew's gospel account, naming and describing these Three Kings. As a result, tradition now holds that Melchior was an old, white-haired Persian scholar who brought gold; Caspar (or "Gaspar") was from India, a ruddy young man bearing frankincense; and Balthasar was a heavily bearded, dark-skinned Babylonian who brought myrrh. The Bible does not mention the number of kings; the assumption of three is based on the number of gifts that were presented to Jesus.[12]

---

12. *The Circle of Seasons-Meeting God in the Church Year*, K.C. Ireton, p. 50

About Those Kings

Our family has been setting up our Nativity scene for over 30 years, and the Wise Men are always there at the manger along with Mary, Joseph and Jesus. This is most likely an inaccurate depiction. Although we don't know exactly *when* the Magi arrived, Scripture records the time frame as "after the birth of Jesus." It would be safe to say it was either sometime within the first year or approximately two years later. Why belabor this distinction of days? It might seem like splitting hairs, but there is a day we celebrate Christ's appearance on the earth to His family and another that marks His appearance to the Gentiles, the rest of the world. They are two separate occasions.

The first day is celebrated by the exchanging of gifts, the other by offering them and expecting nothing in return. Our current Christian worldview often adopts the Magi's example as proof that giving presents is the point of Christmas. But the heart of Epiphany is to recalibrate our Christmas season focus from the pinnacle of a single gift-giving event—the day we celebrate Christ's birth— to look again at what we have already received—God's love and salvation. Taking a second look reveals that in addition to looking at what we receive at Christmas, we can consider what we have to share: the love of God with others.

The celebration of Epiphany provides the opportunity to continue that message of love through our actions and words on into the New Year. So how can we engage our families in this process as we widen our worship beyond just one day, living as Holy Day Ambassadors?

To Epiphany and Beyond

Since I'm no longer in the classroom teaching and I don't have school-aged children around, the fact that Christmas vacation has come to an end does not hold the punch it once did for me. I rarely notice that the neighborhood kids have gone back to school except for one thing—it's January 6 and the resident gnomes have taken the Santa hat off the lion. Yes, we have a concrete lion in our cul de sac flower bed, placed there years ago by some committee or other in an attempt to—what?—beautify our little circle, probably. I always refer to the Lion as Aslan, of course, but my neighbor's children still insist on sneaking out in the dead of night on Christmas Eve, placing a fluffy red and white cap atop his head. *I don't think Aslan would wear a Santa hat.*

Oddly enough, though they are not church-going folks, come Epiphany, no more Santa, just plain Aslan the concrete lion. The hat is gone. I'm sure that's symbolic of something. I'm just not sure what. Aside from removing Santa hats, there are other ways families mark Epiphany in this day and age. Some practices include playing with chalk, lighting candles and feeding camels. *Well, sort of.*

Epiphany follows Twelfth Night on January 5, and some of the traditions overlap. If your Christmas tree is taken down and ornaments are put away, you could consider leaving your Nativity set out and finally introducing the Wise Men (who have been patiently waiting somewhere else in your house) to Mary, Joseph and Jesus. My friend Kay's family leaves their crèche out all the way until Feb. 2, Candlemas, another church year observance. [13]

Perhaps, like me, your evangelical background hasn't provided an opportunity for any particular church practices surrounding Epiphany. In fact, if you've never heard of the feast day until now, you would not be alone. One friend told me that their nondenominational church observes Epiphany with a progressive dinner. That's not exactly a traditional practice, per se, but a modern-day take on the journey of the Wise Men. "We have lanterns everywhere along the way but travel by car across the city to different peoples' houses for appetizer, salad, main course and dessert." *Just like the Wise Men, but without the camels.*

Jane told me, "Our Swiss friends taught us about Three Kings Day on Epiphany. Someone makes a special breakfast pastry, like sweet rolls, and puts a small plastic king in one of them. Whoever gets that rolls is 'king' for a day,

---

13. Candlemas is the last festival in the Christian year that is dated by reference to Christmas. Candlemas falls on February 2 and celebrates the presentation of Christ in the Temple in Jerusalem 40 days after his birth (as Jewish custom required). The day is so called because of the practice of lighting and blessing candles, signifying Jesus as the Light of the World. I can think of another "holiday" we celebrate on Feb. 2. Interesting how we've adopted these church year observances, yes?

but it is the reminder, of course, that Jesus came for all, including the Gentile kings."

My friend Lidia shares, "Epiphany is when I give the last gifts to my kids and tell them about my childhood in Mexico. I explain that I received my own gifts on that day, and since the three Wise Men gave their gifts to Jesus, that's who brought mine. In return, we children left food in our shoes for the wise men's camels, I tell them. Now I practice this with my grandchildren and tell them about the three wise kings."

Now, I have no idea what kind of food camels eat, but the point here is to engage your children in extending the Christmas season beyond just one day and adjusting their focus to include the rest of their world. A story about the Wise Men and their camels might help and could lead to learning about Christmas traditions in other parts of the world.

As Christ's birth weaves its way into all of our days, children and grandchildren will welcome the chance to learn how to have Christmas every day. Of course, there won't be new presents each morning, but they can celebrate Christ's presence in simple ways.

Action Ideas—*Epiphany*

1. *Light up the dark*

   Is the Christ candle still out at your house? If not, you can light one now. The liturgical color of Epiphany is white, but any color will do. Even if you have a single candlestick on your table, you can light it each evening and simply repeat the words:

Candlelighter: "Jesus Christ is the Light of the World."
Respondents: "The light no darkness can overcome."

2. *Learning Opportunity—Memorize a prophecy*
Depending on your children's ages, you and your family might consider memorizing the verses from Isaiah 60.

3. *Dress up like the Magi, and put on a play*
Just like the Nativity story, the arrival of the Three Kings can be a fun story to act out as you teach your children the importance of the kings' arrival. God came first to his Jewish parents; then he appeared to all people. This is a big deal. Have someone write a script; design costumes (old bathrobes come in handy for this). Perform for your friends and family; the possibilities are endless, whether in a homeschool setting or just for fun. Especially if it's a Snow Day.

4. *Chalk the Door*
I remember the first time I saw what looked like hieroglyphics or some strange math written above a doorway in the Ballard neighborhood of Seattle. *What IS that? And how did it get up there? And why? Maybe mathematicians live there …*
My friend Kay enlightened me some time later, telling me the markings were part of a church tradition

of "chalking the door" on the evening of Epiphany. In fact, the next time I visited her house, there was the inscription "20+C+M+B+16" above the front door.

What exactly IS chalking the door?

This practice is a time-honored tradition, possibly related all the way back to biblical times when the Jews marked the lintels above their doorways on Passover. Nowadays, Anglican, Methodist, Presbyterian and Catholic families as well as many other Protestants continue this practice of identifying their homes as a place where God dwells.

The formula for the ritual — adapted for 2018 — is simple: Take chalk of any color and write the following above the entrance of your home: **20 + C + M + B + 18.**

- The 20 at the beginning and the 18 at the end mark the year.
- The letters C, M & B have two meanings. First, they represent the initials of the Magi — Caspar, Melchior and Balthazar — and they also abbreviate the Latin phrase *Christus mansionem benedicat*: "May Christ bless the house."

The letters C, M & B have two meanings

- The "+" signs are crosses in between. Taken together, this inscription is written as a request that Christ bless those homes so marked and a reminder that He remains with those who dwell inside throughout the entire year.

Now it's your turn. Go find that tub of pink and

blue stubby chalk pieces that you used on the sidewalk and give your kids a chance to draw on the house. Oh, and get a ladder.

5. *Bless the House*
When we first moved into our Seattle suburb over 25 years ago, several friends from church came over for a time of prayer after we were settled into our home. We joined together, inviting God's presence to be with us all the days we lived there. Of course, we know the kingdom of God goes with us wherever we are, but a simple ceremony with chalk and prayers is one way to remind ourselves and our families of how we can live that out in our daily lives.

Praying a blessing over your house after you've marked your doorway with chalk is also part of church tradition on Epiphany. Practicing this annually is a way to remind your family of whose you are and how God wants you to live in the world.

Here's an example of what you might pray as you gather your family or friends together:

Dear God, we ask that you would bless all those who enter our home and bless us in turn as we go into the world to share your kingdom through our actions and our words. We make this a special place for you, Jesus, and invite you to be a daily guest in our conversations, our work, our play, our happiness, and especially our sorrows. Thank you for your presence here. Amen.

Of course, as we've said throughout *Living the Season*

Well, you can adopt or adapt this prayer and practice in a way that works for your family. Engage your children in the process by inviting them to pray (or read the prayer). Write your own family prayer.

One Last Thing "As You Go"

The message of Epiphany is that God has appeared to ALL people, Jews and Gentiles alike. We can be like the Wise Men who returned to their homes spreading the news of the King they had seen. Our rejoicing in the Savior, Jesus our King, leads to going out and telling those in our world, too.

As we come and go through our front doors, chalked with the reminder that we have welcomed God into our homes, our lives and conversations give birth to an awareness that we carry God's kingdom with us. We began the Christmas season at the end of November; now, we are in January. Think of Epiphany as the sending-out point into the rest of the year. Don't stop at Christ's birth, but journey into the days that follow. Marking God's entrance into the world and your exit into the same, venture through the door of your home with an attitude that Christ is with you. You have seen the Savior and you want to tell the world.

What will you share as you go, not via camel, but on foot or in the car? How and where will you share God's kingdom of love and redemption into the supermarket, the grocery store, the coffee shop?

Jot some ideas here in this space and let me know what you did; I'd love to hear. Drop me a line? [14]
Start small. Start now.

---

14. Heyjode70@yahoo.com

CHAPTER 8

Conclusion

WRAPPING IT UP

It is one thing for us, in our own time ... to behold the icon. It's quite another to know that all the time the icon is beholding and expecting us, patiently awaiting our arrival.

—*Malcolm Guite*, Waiting on the Word

Enjoying the season of Christmas (not just the day) by changing the way we celebrate begins by adjusting the way we *think*. Thoughts become actions, and actions become a way of life. Our children mimic what we say and model what we do. If we want to see changes in their attitudes and expectations (or our own), the examples must begin with us. *But that takes time.*

> *Thoughts become actions, and actions become a way of life.*

With what you've read in this little book, you can begin to move your family in the direction of rejoicing in *all* the days of Christmas, not just December 25. You can avoid the rush and crush of just one day with that huge crash on the other side. But how do we turn around the expectations, simplify our celebrations and savor the birth of our Savior? Very, very slowly.

Word Play-*expectio*

In this chapter's opening quote, Malcolm Guite says that during the Christmas season, not only are we waiting for God, but He is also expecting us. The root word of *expecting* is the Latin word *expectio*, that is to say, *looking out*.

The root word of expecting is the Latin word expectio, that is to say, looking out.

In the opening chapter, we talked about the traditions of the church year being like the image of a landscape quickly rushing by as we look out the window of a train. Looking *out*, of course, implies looking *for*, and *Living the Season Well* is about looking for our Savior Jesus, waiting through the days of Advent for His arrival, celebrating His birth on Christmas and commemorating His appearance to the rest of the world on Epiphany. Now that we've seen our Savior, we can go and tell the world of His coming. This is the message of Christmas—God is here among us; it's not the presents but His presence that matters.

What Will You Do Now?

In this chapter, I'll briefly review what we've read, recapping the Action Ideas so you may glean from the text. Several choices will be listed for you to begin the small changes, along with some extras added for fun. Circle those you want to try. At the end of the chapter there will be a space to jot them down.

CHAPTER 1-A SUBTLE SHIFT
Unwrapping the Gift of Liturgy

Action Ideas to Consider

1. Make a decision to discuss Christmas season changes with your spouse and/or children.

2. Include the relatives in the conversation. (Bake some cookies first.)

3. Spend some time in prayer, asking God to reveal any needed adjustments.

4. Tell a friend what you've learned from this short book.

CHAPTER 2-ADVENT
Why Waiting Matters

Action Ideas

1. Make an Advent Wreath (or buy one—Goodwill, remember?).

2. Choose a candle lighter for each Sunday.

3. Read the weekly Scripture passages.

4. Keep Nana's daily calendar up, too.

Extra

Plant an amaryllis bulb. I usually buy my bulb when they go on sale at the end of October (if I can remember!).

Engage your kids in unpacking the box, soaking up the growing medium and planting the bulb. This is a simple illustration of keeping your eyes out for the coming blooms (cut out the flower photo on the box and keep it handy to refer to). Granted, just watching the crinkly white globe while it sits in the dirt won't make it bloom, but it is a nice diversion and a remarkable surprise when something so dead-looking springs to life. Talk with your children about waiting patiently even when you can't see something happening. This is the heart of Advent.

CHAPTER 3-GETTING READY
Preparing our Homes, Heads & Hearts

Action Ideas

1. Have children help with decorations in the house and on the tree.

2. Keep the camels and Wise Men somewhere away from the Nativity scene, since Scripture says they came after baby Jesus was born.

3. Discuss gift expectations.

4. Reconsider fasting—putting off, setting aside, laying down.

Extra

Put on a show. The idea is to divert your kids' energy towards something besides all the things they want: Keep them busy with play, like an actual play. *Sort of.* Encourage your children and/or their friends to write a Christmas skit and act it out. (Talk about Learning Opportunity). Maybe they know Dickens' *A Christmas Carol*, or they want to enact the Nativity story from the Bible. Of course, you'll need a playwright, someone to oversee costumes, a director. Some sheep. Or Santas and elves. Or Mary.

The point here is not perfection but engaging your children in something else during the season that will focus them on family, friends and the joy of being together. Giving them language that identifies the heart of the season is as simple as saying, *"It makes me happy to see you _____ [being kind to our neighbor, having fun with your siblings, saying hello to the store clerk] at Christmas; that's what it's all about."*

CHAPTER 4-WHAT ABOUT THE PRESENTS?
Changing the Way We Give

Action Ideas

1. Further those budget discussions.

2. Have teenagers research their gift requests.

3. Channel school-agers' energy into organizing a gift drive at their school.

4. Encourage tweens or teenagers to organize a Christmas lighting contest in your neighborhood, apartments or condos.

5. Have children give away two toys for every one they

want. Make a donation bag and deliver it to a nonprofit that takes donations.

6. Get creative with wish lists—cut out newspaper ads and make a collage; write it out.

7. Encourage children to pray about what they want for Christmas, teaching them that God is ultimately the Source of everything.

8. Rethink your giving and research nonprofits to support.

Extra

Start a piggy bank fund. Choose a nonprofit to support—Compassion International, World Vision—or a cause you believe in. Some other nonprofit ideas are listed in the Appendix.

CHAPTER 5-CHRISTMAS
Savoring the Celebration (Santa Claus AND Jesus)

Action Ideas

1. Choose a child to light the Christ Candle on Christmas Eve.

2. Have someone read the prophecy of Christ's birth in Luke 1:26-38.

3. Light the Christ candle, and read the story of Jesus' birth in Luke Chapter 2 (vv. 1-21) on Christmas morning.

4. Have children keep inching the camels and/or Wise Men closer to your Nativity scene each day.

5. Choose a child to put baby Jesus in the manger on Christmas morning.

Extra

Learning Opportunity: Have children research Christmas celebrations around the world. How are they similar to your own? How are they different?

CHAPTER 6-THE 12 DAYS
Spreading out the Holiday Energy

Action Ideas

1. Spread out the giving of gifts.

2. Put away the greenery and decorations a little each day.

3. Read through the Christmas cards—who are they from? Pray for them or write a note.

4. Keep photo cards as prayer cards to use during the year.

5. Remember the Wise Men and camels? Keep them moving.

6. **Learning Opportunity:** Read Shakespeare's play *Twelfth Night*.

Extra

Encourage the observance of a New Year's Eve service at your church. Even to the unchurched, New Year's Eve is a time to begin, when people look forward to a new start. The church calendar also contains a feast proclaiming January 1 as the Feast of the Circumcision of the Lord, a Christian celebration of the circumcision of Jesus in accordance with Jewish tradition. Jesus' circumcision has traditionally been seen as the first time the blood of Christ was shed, and many churches observe New Year's Eve with a Communion service. Suggest to your pastor or youth leader that you observe New Year's Eve this way.

For evangelical congregations, this might be a big leap, but it makes wonderful sense. Many pastors might welcome a way to refocus the festivities by including an intentional, reflective time for their church body on New Year's Eve.

CHAPTER 7-EPIPHANY
Telling the World About our King

Action Ideas

1. Pray a blessing over your house and chalk the door.

2. Have kids dress up like the Magi and put on a play.

3. Memorize the prophecy about the Kings in Isaiah 60:1-6.

4. "As You Go" activities—on 3 x 5 cards, write down the ways you can take the news of Jesus with you wherever you go. Keep the cards in a basket by the front door.

Extra

- Consider introducing the practices surrounding Epiphany to your church, with either your lead pastor or children's pastor. These are simple ways to ask, "Now that our Savior has come, what do we do? We tell people!" The lead pastor could bring a message incorporating these new (to you) ideas.

- Kids can make "As You Go" activity cards in Sunday School or pretend to feed the Wise Men's camels and learn about Christmas celebrations around the world.
- Volunteer to organize a progressive dinner for your church or fellowship to symbolize the Magi's journey to see Jesus.

You now have 35 ways to slow down, savor and simplify Christmas. What might you try? Jot down your ideas here, one for each chapter, or go back first and read those notes you scribbled in the margins.

1.

2.

3.

4.

5.

6.

7.

We began this journey through the arc of days from Advent, four Sundays before Christmas, through Epiphany on January 6. If we include Candlemas in February, we have an even wider piece of the year's circle referenced by the Christmas season. The day we celebrate Christ's birth is just one resting point in the cycle through the church year. Christmas shares nearly equal importance with the other anchor of our Christian faith, Easter. So, rather than being the peak of a mountain, we can think of the holiday—Holy Day—as a time we pass *through* each year. *Christmas (and Easter) are times that change us even as the times change.*

Christmas is more than just the arrival of light into our world during the darkest days of winter; we can widen our worship beyond one day, carrying that light all through the year. I pray as you look back over what you've read you will consider slowing down, simplifying and savoring all the days you count while *living the season well.*

I will end with this quote from *The Chronicles of Narnia,* which captures the heart of this book—Christmas is not the end of the season, but merely the beginning:

The term is over: the holidays have begun. The dream is ended: this is the morning ... But for them it was only the beginning of the real story. All their life in this world and all their adventures in Narnia had only been the cover and the title page: now at last they were beginning Chapter One of the Great Story which no one on earth has read: which goes on forever: in which every chapter is better than the one before.

—C. S. Lewis, The Last Battle

Appendix
Free Downloads on jodyleecollins.com/books

Books for Families & Children

1. *All Creation Waits: The Advent Mystery of New Beginnings*—Gayle Boss

2. *Home for Christmas: Stories for Young and Old*—Henry Van Dyke

3. *Manger*—Lee Bennett Hopkins et al (a poetry collection for children)

4. *One Wintry Night*—Ruth Graham Bell

5. *Santa's Favorite Story*—Hisako Aoki, Ivan Gantschev

6. *Song of the Stars*—Sally Lloyd Jones

7. *The Story of the Other Wiseman*—Henry Van Dyke (1895). Free online

8. *The Gift of the Magi*—O. Henry, Illus. by Lisbeth Zwerger

9. *The Man Who Invented Christmas* (Charles Dickens)—Les Standiford. Also a movie, released in 2017, with Christopher Plummer as Scrooge

10. *The Twenty-four Days Before Christmas*
Madeleine L'Engle

Books for Grown-ups

1. *31 Days of Christmas: A Devotional for Advent* (The 31-Day Series, Vol. 2)—Susan Shipe

2. *Come, Lord Jesus: The Weight of Waiting: 25 Daily Readings for Advent*—Kris Camealy

3. *Comfort Ye My People: The Real World Meets Handel's Messiah, 26 Readings for Advent*—Kay Bruner

4. *The Glorious Impossible, Illustrations from frescoes by Giotto*—Madeleine L'Engle

5. *The Gospel of Christmas: Reflections for Advent*—Patty Kirk

6. *Touching Wonder: Recapturing the Awe of Christmas*—John Blase

7. *Waiting on the Word: A Poem a Day for Advent, Christmas and Epiphany*—Malcolm Guite

8. *Watch for the Light: Readings for Advent & Christmas*—Various

9. *The Advent of the Lamb of God*—Russ Ramsey

10. *When Holidays Hurt: Finding Hidden Hope Amid Pain and Loss*—Bo Stern

Christmas Resources

1. *Jesse Trees*: The Jesse Tree represents Jesus' family tree. It takes us through that first long Advent, which lasted from the Fall to the Incarnation, with a collection of Scripture meditations to prepare for the coming of Christ at Christmas. **Free resources at joyfilledfamily.com.** Google the term and you'll find all kinds of other ideas.

2. *JoyWares*: Jesse Tree Ornaments, Cradle to Cross Advent Wreaths – joywares.ca. "Our vision is to make beautiful heirloom JoyWares for generations of families, inviting families into keeping joyful, grateful company with Jesus in their everyday lives. A portion of all profits of JoyWares reduces poverty in third world nations such as Haiti, African countries and many others." –owner Caleb Voskamp

3. *Lighted Windows: An Advent Calendar for a World in Waiting*—Margaret Silf

4. *The Advent Coloring Calendar*— Gayle Boss, Paraclete Press

5. *The Christmas Star from Afar*—A Game That Celebrates the True Meaning of Christmas 16-piece set: hardcover book and full wooden Nativity set. $34.99

Nonprofit Organizations

1. Lulu Tree—*thelulutree.com*. Lulu partners with pastors and community leaders in villages across Uganda and Sierra Leone, seeking to equip families through their churches. Their work is also supported by their online shop, selling clothing and jewelry made by "Lulu Mamas."

2. Preemptive Love—*preemptivelove.org*. This coalition works directly with the people of the Middle East—Syria, Iraq, Libya—in "unmaking violence," supporting the work of physicians, volunteers and the local people in bringing healing to their countries. They exist because of generous donations and also through an online shop of items made by local people.

3. First Aid Arts—*firstaidarts.org*. Leaders since 2010 in bringing effective arts-based healing resources to trauma survivors, particularly those rescued from human trafficking, and those who care for them.

4. REST Ministries—*iwantrest.com*. REST: Real Escape from the Sex Trade is an independent 501(c)(3) Washington State Charitable Nonprofit Organization, founded in November 2009 to help support and rescue trafficked women and youth.

5. Sew Powerful—*sewpowerful.org*. Sew Powerful exists to combat extreme poverty in a very challenging place called Ngombe Compound in Lusaka Zambia.

They do that by equipping community members with jobs as well as training, tools and technical skills to make what they call *"Purposeful Products,"* *training African women in sewing and small business building.*

Acknowledgments

It is one thing to announce to the world (well, close friends and family), "I'm going to write a book!" and quite another to follow through. I thought I knew what the process entailed, but there's a kind of grace in that saying, "you don't know what you don't know." For all those who came alongside me to offer encouragement, cheerleading, hand-holding, prayer and support, "thank you" seems an inadequate pair of words.

I couldn't have begun the process without Kimberlee Ireton's taking my book proposal and lovingly penciling it into something usable. Thank you for validating my efforts and clapping when I finished. To my faithful blog readers, thank you for staying with me from the beginning and following along. To the gifted Glory Writers around the world, thanks for believing in me, cheering me on and weighing in on the perfect cover—you rock. William Johnson, your giftedness in illustration and design astonish me—you make this book look amazing. (Thank you, Leah, for helping with the smashed box).

Early manuscript readers—Shanna Mallon, Heather Lefebvre, Glenda Childers, Adrienne Whitmore, Jennifer Ferguson, Robyn Field and the queen of all that is

Christmas, Nancy Franson, much of what you shared with me is in these pages. I'm so grateful for your inestimable help. A special thanks to poet and friend of writers Laurie Klein, who gently pushed me to dump out all the pieces of my first draft and rearrange them into something new. I also owe a debt of gratitude to the remarkable Emily Allen who poured out creative marketing suggestions from her ever flowing fountain of ideas.

To two editors—Laura Brown, who helped me see the veins in the leaves on the trees in the forest, and Andi Cumbo-Floyd, who helped me see the forest from the sky—my words became so much better with your help. Thank you.

To my precious family—Aaron and Courtney, Leah and William, Hanan, Peter, Abigail, Luke and Paul, my siblings and their spouses—it was joy to weave the gifts of who you are into these pages.

My husband Bill constantly supported me, scaffolding my days and picking up way more slack in our home than is reasonable for one person. Thank you, honey, for telling everyone who asked, "My wife's writing a book about Christmas. You should buy it!" Your enthusiasm is a gift. I love you.

Every time I mentioned this work in conversation or prayer, I felt a little Holy Spirit nudge that it wasn't "my book" but the book God gave me to write. I pray His message—to slow down and savor the gift of the Savior—will be illuminated by this earthly messenger.

CPSIA information can be obtained
at www.ICGtesting.com
Printed in the USA
FSHW021949060919
61805FS